BELIEVE
NATION

Believe Nation: The Belief of a Nation is published under Mission Books, sectionalized division under Di Angelo Publications INC.

MISSION BOOKS

An imprint of Di Angelo Publications. Believe Nation: The Belief of a Nation

Di Angelo Publications 4265 San Felipe #1100
Houston, Texas, 77027
www.diangelopublications.com

Library of Congress cataloging-in-publications data

Believe Nation: The Belief of a Nation Downloadable via Kindle, iBooks and NOOK.

Library of Congress Registration Hardback

ISBN: 978-1-942549-87-1

Developmental Editing: Elizabeth Geeslin Zinn
Internal Layout: Kimberly James

1. Business & Economics -- Entrepreneurship
2. Business & Economics -- Mentoring & Coaching
3. Business & Economics -- Motivational
4. Self Help -- Personal Growth -- Success
5. Religion -- Christian Living -- Leadership & Mentoring
6. Religion -- Christian Living -- Professional Growth

United States of America with int. Distribution.

BELIEVE NATION

THE BELIEF OF A NATION

DAVID IMONITIE

CONTENTS

INTRODUCTION

PART ONE

PART TWO

PART THREE

PART FOUR

INTRODUCTION

BELIEVE NATION

Believe Nation is the most powerful achievement platform on the planet. Through Believe Nation, we teach and develop the commitment it takes to be ready to rise above the noise in our own heads, and in the world, in order to achieve greatness. We are a global collective designed to help you create the life of your dreams. It's a 24/7 platform that serves as motivational fuel for your dreams and brings together a coalition of people who are rcady to rise up in their lives. The aim is to personally inspire you into action that will transform your life.

Believe Nation is where you will practice daily success habits. There are two sides to success: the mental, spiritual side, and the strategies and techniques side. When I first began, I had no idea that the mental aspect of things was the key to accelerating my success. After reflecting on what it took to get me where I am, my personal belief is that the ratio is actually 90-95% mental to 1-10% strategies and techniques.

This book follows the lessons given on Believe Nation's platform, and gives you supplemental information and training to teach you how to truly believe in and attain all of your goals for your life. As your millionaire mentor and guide, I want to thank you for bringing me into your world. It is an incredible honor for me to share my knowledge with you. As an exclusive citizen of Believe Nation, you have access to my world-class training, which includes everything ranging from creating empowering beliefs to my secret success formula that never fails. I'm also going to teach you the seven-figure habits of a seven-figure earner with the power of your environment, repetitious information, associations (power in proximity) and what you actually experience.

People rarely ever go out and experience what it is they want; they experience what it is they already have. They talk themselves out of believing they can have more than what they currently accept for themselves. With this book, in conjunction with the Believe Nation digital platform, I am aiming to inspire one billion people on this planet into their own greatness. I want to impact one billion people with encouragement, hope and love.

Everyone, regardless of their status or background, was born with the ability to believe their way to success. Each lesson breaks down how to fully believe in your own success and turn your dreams into your reality.

With this book, you are given the tools to create a new comfort zone with your experiences. Most people are tricked by their current situation into thinking that the way things are is the only way things can be for them, and they start making "I can't" statements.

I want each one of you reading this to know that you can live an exceptional life.

Some say that success is relative. This mindset ends up sinking into your thought process and it will hinder your ability to achieve what is actually possible for you. Your ability to achieve success is 90% mental. The other 10% is based on the action you take to create the bridge from where you are when you begin to the point of achieving your success.

I know exactly what it feels like to be in your current position, and I can show you exactly what I did to get to where I am today. I want you to be fully engaged in what Believe Nation teaches because what you will begin to realize is that the more you play, the more you'll win.

Throughout this book, you will be charged with daily actions to move you along in your journey through built-in accountability, along with the actual source and purpose of following my teachings on achieving success. I've designed it this way because Believe Nation cares about you and we want you to succeed. You're not in this alone—along with reading this book, Believe Nation's platform allows you to have access to other action-takers like yourself, and you will have the opportunity to learn from me through monthly in-depth, live training.

You're going to learn how to get past your insecurities. You'll learn there is no perfect industry and that there is a wide variety of success and failure in every occupation. Because it's not about what company or industry you're currently in—it's about who you are and it's about being aware of the power that is within your human spirit.

All of the features within Believe Nation have been designed to move you towards your goal one small step at a time. Taking one step forward every day and not giving up is exactly how I've achieved every single goal in my life. I went from being a college dropout and working in the retail industry to multi-millionaire status. Now I inspire millions of people throughout the world. You can do what I did. In fact, you can do *more*. See, every good mentor wants to see their protégés go even further than themselves, and I want that for you because when you rise, we all rise.

The world becomes better because of the greatness you express. I'm so excited that you're reading this book. Your life is about to radically change for the better. If you take the actions suggested in this book and make your commitment to your desires non-negotiable, it is very well possible that your life will soon be completely different—even six months from now...or nine days from now! But I know with assurance that twelve months from now, your life will look completely different.

My goal is to inspire more than one billion people into their own unique greatness and I need your help to achieve this ambitious aim. If you have a friend, a family member, a colleague, or someone you care about in your life who needs this type of information on a regular basis, I strongly encourage you to share it with them. If they have a desire for more in their lives, then please, I implore you to share Believe Nation with them.

I couldn't have truly thrived without learning the success habits I share in this book and remaining disciplined in them. I want you to learn how to create success habits by creating a winning environment even while the world around you is scared. In fact, you can't truly thrive without learning how to develop your success habits and having incredible discipline around them.

Anyone can get free access to Believe Nation's platform just like you. By sharing your BelieveNation.com referral link, you get credit for a friend's referral—and trust me, a lot comes with that credit. In the meantime, I hope you will commit to listening to the available audios and trainings. Listen to them multiple times. Remember, it takes repetition to rewire your brain for success!

The first action I want you to take from this book is to become a citizen of Believe Nation and introduce yourself to the other citizens on the site. Go ahead and post your picture on there. Make it your profile pic. I really want to personally get to know you. I will be popping in and out to read your comments and I want you to be sure to introduce yourself. I want you to follow me on all other social media platforms as well in order to help saturate your social media experience with posts that are helpful or inspiring to you. Remember, you are a champion in your life, but you've got to **conceive** it, you've got to **believe** it, and then you'll **achieve** it.

FORMULATE YOUR WAY TO SUCCESS

Formulas give you a way to break things down. Throughout this book and on Believe Nation, you'll find that I use formulas to explain techniques. *Formula* simply means ingredients—the ingredients you need in order to accomplish goals and create success in life. Formulas allow you to map out your success regardless of what is going on in your world.

MY STORY

My story is not a common one. That's one of the main reasons I started Believe Nation.

Growing up, I was taught to go to school, get good grades, graduate and go out and get a good job. I tried that. I started off just like anyone else as a kindergartener and eventually went to college. I left college as a sophomore—

and that didn't come with a degree. I realized that this was not my path to success.

Like many children who grow up in a traditional household, my parents were my very first mentors. My dad was a professional athlete, later becoming involved in ministry. My mom was an avid fan of the great self-help authors from years past. We had stacks of their books around the house that she'd collected—works ranging from Bob Proctor and Zig Ziglar to Tony Robbins.

Those books, and my mom's interest in them, had a huge influence on my mindset and life. Once I got into the first, I devoured their information over and over again. The ability to emulate someone else is actually priceless. You can take a trait, a habit, or a lesson from them and add to your personal portfolio. No one can ever take knowledge away from you, so once you acquire information—whether it be from books, research on the internet or listening to videos or audiobooks—that information is yours for all time to use as you see fit.

I technically became an entrepreneur at sixteen years old. When a person first gets started on this journey, they don't necessarily know anything about belief systems, desires, or goals—I didn't at first. These are learned along the way. People will often say, "If I only knew then what I know now..." As the old saying goes, hindsight is 20/20.

However, there are ways to bypass wishing you'd known everything when you began your journey to success.

I eventually left college and went into retail. I had thirty-two credits after four years of schooling and I was still only credited as a sophomore! I had learned a little about sales and wanted to make money. Not long after leaving college, at the age of twenty-one, I was introduced to the industry of network marketing, but didn't have any success. I worked with that company for two years and struggled for the duration of those two years. But I took a lot of knowledge from that experience and met some good people. I got out of networking for about six months after that.

I was living with my dad and had a job coaching tennis with him when I was reintroduced to the industry. The second time, the juices started really flowing for me. After two years and four months in that company, I failed—but I learned even more. I was also introduced to one of my first important mentors through that experience, so failure wasn't all that bad for me—the trick was that *I fell up*, not down.

I was introduced to a business model that completely changed my life. It opened me up to learning about business, entrepreneurship and leadership. More importantly, it exposed me to deep levels of personal self-development. This allowed me to create a whole new vision for my life.

The Bible says faith without works is dead. That means that you can have the mental and spiritual side of achieving success in place (faith), but if you don't apply the skills and strategies (work)—even if it's the smaller portion of the success pie—you won't achieve your goals. Your skills and strategies are defined by the actions you take toward your success. Your implementation of skills is applicable to every aspect of your business. Through my personal development, I learned the definition of the faith I needed to succeed.

After practicing self-development, learning how to properly visualize my goals, and studying the new business model I had been given, I thought I would try my hand at business. For the first four-and-a-half—almost five—years, I had no monetary success whatsoever. Honestly, looking back I really have no idea how I stuck it out. I just kept going. Deep down inside of me, I knew that one day I would win if I just stayed in the game.

I understood that every time I fell, even if I fell seven times, I would get back up that eighth time. And that eighth time for me was when I turned twenty-seven, the year I would become a millionaire. The last two-and-a-half years of that journey, I went from living with my father—sleeping on a twin-sized bed and having only $1,000 to my name—to earning over a million dollars. Since then, I've gone on to duplicate my success exponentially.

In the following lessons, I'm going to walk you through weekly action steps to help you create the life you truly desire and deserve. You can also learn from me by watching videos on BelieveNation.com. It's important that you understand and *believe* that this sort of success can also be your story. It starts with belief in yourself, your greatness and your future. No matter what is showing up in your life at present, I encourage you to commit right now to yourself that you will never, ever give up.

"I can only fly with you if I'm flying behind you. And eventually, I will fly without you." That's a very significant saying for me. The skills that have helped me evolve, and will allow me to continue to evolve, are the skills you're going to learn—and it's always been that way. Whatever skills were important to me at a given time have helped me reach the next level—even if, from the outside looking in, it is not obvious that those skills would carry over. Nothing is ever useless. It just has to be put into action. What you will learn in this book are the skills you need to succeed, but more so, you will learn about who you are becoming.

This is how champions live—they truly commit to winning. Commit yourself to winning right now, and care enough about your goals and your dreams to make that commitment. I want you to give it everything that you have. I promise you that it will pay off in the end.

PART ONE

LESSON ONE
THRIVING

Are you ready to make this daily success habit a real part of your life? Are you ready to latch on to the right emotional state and maintain it? Are you ready to thrive? Remind yourself, "I can really get through this."

Disbelief in your ability to have your desire, and being attached to the feeling of not having it, is the source of any failure you perceive.

Let me explain what that means so that it's crystal clear. Everyone has heard the words of encouragement out there for manifesting dreams and desires. It's easy to hear, "Just imagine you already have what you want, and you'll get it!" One of the obstacles in simply having your desire in your mind is that it becomes an **attachment**. When we get attached to things—ideas, beliefs, even people—we oftentimes don't know how to not check in on them all the time, and we overwhelm our system with our attention! You've got to control where your attention goes and make sure your attention isn't being expressed through attachment. Attachment comes from a fear-based pattern of knowing that lack is a possibility. When we know deep down that there is a possibility we could lack that which we desire, we develop an attachment to it based on that fear.

It's important to understand the root that the word attachment comes from. It's more than just a dictionary definition. Remember, words create things—so the source of a word, its etymology—can be just as important as its dictionary definition. From studying one of the original ancient concepts of attachment, we can see that it is just as important to understand ***detachment***. The ancient view of detachment comes from the understanding of our view of reality. They teach the importance of the present—existing in the moment. You can't be attached or worried about the past or the future. The concept of detachment is to not worry about the past or future, but only the present reality you actually sense.

Detachment is an extremely important part of what it means to have faith. To have faith, you've got to detach yourself from worry. Think about what it means to worry. I don't want you to think about something you might actually worry about, but think about something someone else has worried about and made you aware of recently. More often than not, they're worried about something that either has already happened and is in the past, or something in the future that hasn't even happened to them.

Belief works for you based on how well you develop your ability to detach from what you've attached yourself to. When I tell you what you want is already yours, I'm not telling you to not attach yourself to the belief in the sense of making it part of your desire. What I mean is to detach yourself from any worry about not ever having it in your past and your fear of lacking it in your future. That's what attachment and detachment are actually about.

Furthermore, belief has caveats to it. Just as easy as it might be for you to read this and begin understanding what it means to actually, fully believe, you can also sabotage yourself with belief. Your biggest opponent is often a belief—usually buried deep down inside you—that you won't actually fully realize your desire. Belief works that way, too. If you have even the slightest notion within you in your belief system that it is possible for you to *not* get what you want, then you've planted a seed that is only going to grow.

The power of belief is like a muscle that you have to build. Just like our muscles repair themselves and develop while we sleep, our belief can be nurtured and grow while we rest. This is why it's so important to inundate your mind with good audios or books. The last thing you read, listen to or think about before you go to sleep should be empowering your ability to fully believe. If the last thing you do at night is scroll social media and feed your mind with notions that you don't have what other people are claiming to have, you're sabotaging your belief efforts.

Although you need to feel the right emotions in order to know your desire, belief and faith to be true, your subconscious doesn't deal with emotions. It doesn't argue with the commands your conscious desires give it; it just takes the information you give it and forms your waking reality from that. This is why it is so important that your conscious state—where all the components of your desire, your belief in your desire and your faith reside—are not harboring negativity. You'll unknowingly feed that negativity to your subconscious.

An example of how your subconscious operates with no emotion can be seen anytime you've seen hypnosis. People just come up with facts when they're hypnotized because the hypnotist is accessing the person's subconscious.

Another way to understand our subconscious response to the outside world is by examining how our mind works when we drive. We are actually hypnotized when we drive a car. We don't think about slowing down and stopping at a yellow light that turns red. We do it almost robotically because we've trained our subconscious to maneuver the car in those specific ways when we see those colors. Therefore, our subconscious is reacting to our present reality experienced through our senses. Our subconscious doesn't get emotional about it or understand any emotions involved in the process. It simply is what it is, so it reacts how it has been trained to react. Now, imagine training it to react to obtain your desires! Understand that the exact same principle is at play.

This faith in your subconscious will help you manage the issue of the perceived time it takes to actually see your desire in your reality. Each goal we have includes steps that are, more often than not, designed around a man-made timeline, and your subconscious recognizes that, so you don't have to attach yourself to worry about time as you understand it.

Through reading this and becoming a part of Believe Nation, I want you to learn the shortcuts to constructing, or reconstructing, broken, subconscious faith. It takes practice, and it takes letting go of those old belief systems under which your subconscious has been operating. Imagine if you had started believing this way when you were a child? You can start now and make up for it.

All of our thoughts are generated from our subconscious beliefs, and these thought patterns flow through our mind rapidly and can sometimes feel like we can't control them—but you can. Start retraining your subconscious by responding to every thought you catch in your mind with conscious faith. People who meditate, whether for religious purposes or simply as a personal practice, have learned to do this by acknowledging their thoughts as they come and releasing them...not dwelling on them. Because even if you have a negative thought slip in, you can train your subconscious not to react to that negative thought by acknowledging it, letting the thought go, and replacing it with a thought that comes from your faith.

"Let go and let God," is a phrase we've heard thrown around over the years. It's important to understand what it really means. Too many people relinquish their control over their lives; they have their desires and hopes and say "It's in God's hands now," refusing to take action, maintain their faith, or even understand what "It's in God's hands" actually translates to for us human beings. They think of God as only an outside source, not something they can access from within. If you take, "Let go and let God," and understand it with God being one and the same as I Am, just as He told Moses, then you'll realize what it means. Let go of worry, let your I Am shift this present reality into one that recognizes your desires and beliefs.

It's easier for people to limit themselves by only understanding "let go" and stopping there, assuming "and let God" means that it's totally out of their hands and they don't need to take any action. That is why they don't see results. That's why people give up on desires.

Giving up a desire shouldn't be an option anywhere within your subconscious. So many of us have been taught from a young age to focus on the probability of *not* getting what we want. If you were raised that way, you're going to have to practice merging your conscious self with your I Am power. Any notion you have that failure is likely to occur for you is embedded deeply from a young age. That may not change overnight. Practice changing this belief just like you'd practice shooting a basketball or playing an instrument.

If you continue letting thoughts of your probability of success or failure into your belief system and faith, you're living double-minded. You're trying to have full faith and belief in your desire while at the same time maintaining a space for self-doubt to fester. Even the best multitasker can't fully concentrate on two things at once.

People are often happy to say, "I'm just surviving," when someone asks how they're doing. There's nothing wrong with surviving. I looked up the definition of surviving. It means to exist. It means that you survived this pandemic. You survived the financial crisis. Surviving is essential and it is commendable. But when you're just existing, you're not thriving. Let us look at the definition of *thrive*.

To thrive means to grow; it means to develop. Survival, on the other hand, means only to exist...to be intact. That's what a lot of people are doing right now. They are existing. They are quarantined. They are intact.

That's not what we want our goal to be. We're looking to grow. We're looking to develop. The best part of the thrive definition is that it states when you are thriving, you are prospering and flourishing. The key word in the definition that we are going to focus on here is *flourishing*. When you are flourishing, you are not feeling out of control. When you are flourishing, you are not in fear. When you are flourishing, you don't have anxiety.

Because it is such a key word, let's look up what *flourish* means. Its definition states "for a person, animal or any living organism to grow or to develop in a healthy or vigorous way."

Discovering this definition blew my mind when I read it, especially as it relates to a particularly favorable environment. This has absolutely nothing to do with survival mode or just existing. Rather it means that you are moving, you are growing in a vigorous way. In other words, regardless of the situation, regardless of what's going on in the world, "I'm thriving right now."

So that's what you have to say to yourself: "I'm

flourishing right now." It's imperative that you not only say it, but you imagine what flourishing looks like in every aspect of your life and allow yourself to experience how that feels.

Regardless of whatever is going on in your current reality, regardless of the pandemic, regardless of the financial crisis in the world, regardless of the stock market, regardless of what's going on in trading, regardless of what's going on with your family or your personal life—you must understand what it means for you to be flourishing. There might be a health concern or a death in your family, but regardless of that, it's important for you to speak the words: "I'm thriving, I'm flourishing right now," because regardless of what exists in front of your five physical senses, you are in a favorable environment.

When I realized this, I thought, "This is what we have been teaching for many, many years." Your environment must be favorable to the destination you desire. So, in our imaginary coaching session, I'm sitting down with you right now. You say that you want to make $10,000 per month. I then ask you about what environment you are in. In other words, have you created an environment that's favorable to your desired outcome?

Let's look up another definition, this time the word

environment. It is defined as "the surroundings or conditions in which a person, animal or plant lives or operates in." If you just look up the meaning and origin of some words, you'll be astonished at what you will find out.

My question for you is this: In terms of a previous goal that has been tossed aside, have you allowed the surroundings and conditions of your world to be the dominant part of your environment?

How did you let that occur?

You watch CNN. You watch Fox News. You're constantly listening to what's going on in the world. I live in this same world too, but I'm not **of** this world. That's the belief you've got to have. I may live in this world—but I'm not of this world. I'm of another world; a completely different world.

I'm in the heavens—that's where I live. My body may be here, but my spirit doesn't operate based on what the world says. If I operated based on what the world says, I shouldn't be where I am today. Based on what the world says, at some point, we couldn't even host a live session on Believe Nation. None of it would exist.

Let me further explain what is meant by this. If I tell you I'm in the heavens—in my own world—what I mean is that although my body and my senses exist in the regular world you see before you, my mental state exists in my own "heaven," so to speak. Mentally, I exist in a world where I am flourishing. Everything in my world is set up to pave the way for my continued success in the other world, which I share with everyone physically. I have the ultimate say-so over what I experience in this world of mine. Do people still die? Yes, but I view the loss much differently than I would in the "real" world that everyone seems to suffer in. Do people still get into car accidents? Are there still tragedies in the news? Yes, and although I am connected to all of this through my existence, I'm not simply just surviving through all of it; rather, I'm thriving during all of it. I don't let the outside world define me.

In every situation, it is important for you to ***find a way***. What's the way?

I don't care about what your family says. I don't care about what your friends say. Here's what I do care about: I care about you ***thriving***. I care about you developing. I care about you growing.

The one thing that I've learned is to never look at the problem and speak about the problem. When you speak about a problem, you're speaking it into your reality. Of course, you can look at the problem *and observe the problem*. Naturally, I see when there is a problem. I don't just walk around blindly, not acknowledging real issues! The difference herein lies with how I speak about a problem. I don't give the problem more life than it has by making itself known. I don't speak more of it into existence. I don't feed it my energy by dwelling on it. The words I choose to use to deal with problems and challenges are very specific.

If I find that I've got a challenge, then I need to speak to it using words that don't bring me down into it. If it's darkness, I've got to speak light. My environment, my surroundings, the condition that I'm in has to be favorable.

You might want to ask me, "How do I go about doing that, David? How do I go about creating the right environment? Creating the right surroundings?" You start with the simple concepts of **pictures** and **words**. You need to print out your written goals so that you can surround yourself with those words. Your aim is to create the surroundings and conditions for where it is that you want to go, and what end result you have in mind for yourself.

I could pay attention and give mental energy to all of the doom and the gloom that is going on right now in the world. I could pay attention to my past mistakes and dwell on them, thinking, "If only I had said this instead of that." That's what a lot of people do. They pay attention to their past failures, not understanding that it is their past failures that have allowed them to get to where they are today. Your past failures is what is going to allow you to grow and see a better tomorrow. Therefore, surrounding yourself with words and imagery that direct you to your desired end result is a form of conditioning. This will create a healthy pattern in order for you to manage your emotions and stay on the right track.

LESSON TWO

MANAGING YOUR EMOTIONS DURING TIMES OF STRESS

Simply showing up during scary times is half the battle. Showing up and maintaining control over yourself—your emotions—is powerful. It is what it means to be thriving. As of the writing of this book, we are living in some interesting times right now.

There are some really scary things happening all around the world. Our economy is in a timeout in a lot of ways. We are charting uncharted waters like never before in our lifetime. But guess what? People have gone before us and have gone through worse times than this. The times in which we live are no excuse as a hindrance to achieving our dreams. Everyone who came before us would make the same statement: times are hard. We're living in a frightening age. There is economic instability. The key to overcoming the times you live in is to only nurture the emotions that benefit you. Sadness doesn't benefit you. Living in a state of fear doesn't help you gain anything. It's one thing to experience these emotions; it's another to dwell on them.

This isn't our first rodeo as humans. Our ancestors made it through some incredibly dark times. God created us to survive during short periods of difficulty and thrive for centuries. It's absolutely critical now that no matter what, you begin to put your focus on thriving versus surviving. When you are in survival mode, you are literally in a state of fight-or-flight. You're fueled by anxiety, you feel defensive and you're stuck in the mode of sending negative messages to your brain over and over again, telling it there is a major threat around you that is trying to harm you.

Thousands of years ago, fear and negativity in humans looked like being out in the wilderness and encountering a predator. The fight-or-flight anxiety would rush through our veins and tighten our chest in order to alert us to the immediate threat and help us save ourselves.

Now, in the advanced, abundant world we live in, fear and negativity look a whole lot different. Maybe you are out driving and someone slams on their brakes. The anxious fight-or-flight sensation fills you up as you instantly react. You could be watching your child at the park and see they are about to fall, or you see your child running away from you into a crowd or toward a busy street. These are short situations that require fast action. They are split seconds, not days or months. They quickly churn up fear, anxiety and negative emotions—but it is only temporary. You feel immediate gratitude when you react in time to avoid whatever perils were closing in.

What we're living in right now, this worldwide pandemic, will take many months to pass. This is not a situation that requires your brain to be in an active state of fight-or-flight. Thus, remaining in this state will only move you backwards, away from your desired outcomes. Getting stuck in survival mode leads to anxiety, fear, and greed. When even one of your fears is placed in the driver's seat, it will run all of your decisions.

Long-term survival mode leads not only to health problems, but also money problems and relationship problems. In turn, those will lead to business problems. We do not know how long this pandemic is going to last. We do not know what is going to happen with the economy. However, I can promise you this: you cannot wait for things to get better and then take action. You must consciously make a decision to thrive right now. It is going to require a massive effort mentally and emotionally.

Take the Law of Inverse Transformation, first penned by Doctor Joseph Murphy. It states that if what you desire would give a particular emotion, a specific happiness or satisfaction, then experiencing these feelings can also spur the desire into existence. For example, if you want to drive a certain type of car, then within yourself, produce the same emotional response you'd have if you already possessed that car. By creating that emotional response within yourself, you create the reality of owning that car. While I am putting my own spin and perspective on this Law, this is the exact same concept I want you to learn. You must truly believe you have what you desire by feeling that you already possess it.

He developed this concept from the scientific law of the inverse square. The scientific law states that the intensity of light or other linear waves radiating from a point source (energy per unit of area perpendicular to the source) is inversely proportional to the square of the distance from the source. Therefore, an object of the exact same size that is twice as far away receives only one quarter of the energy.

Murphy assumed that if this law worked for energy in the form of light, it could work for energy created in the mind. Thus, he began putting himself in the emotional state of already having the desired outcome, and in following the scientific law, he achieved the desired outcome.

In principle, Murphy's notion is the same concept of having love and gratitude for what you want no matter what is going on around you in the world. Maintaining the right emotional mindset is absolutely paramount to getting what you desire.

Right now, there is an enormous opportunity to show up and make a difference in the world. It's the perfect opportunity to support your family or level yourself up. Throughout history, there are times when millionaires and billionaires are made, and those times are right now. You will only see this opportunity if you can put things into perspective—the correct perspective. When you begin to look through the eyes and lens of gratitude, you will begin to see the opportunity that is all around you.

During times like these, I'm very careful not to allow excessive negativity into my brain. I know what kind of effect dwelling on those negative emotions will reap for me. I avoid lingering on any excessive negativity by cutting out known sources of it. I don't watch the news. I don't pay attention to the headlines or the media. I change the subject when I'm talking to friends and family members who are obsessing about the virus. I actively choose to see the abundance and opportunity. I'm choosing to be a force for good today. The decision is yours as well.

It may have never occurred to you to look up what the meaning of the word *emotion* is. *Emotion* is a natural, instinctive state of mind deriving from one's circumstances, mood, or relationship with others. I personally apply the meaning by how I am moved. I am naturally and instinctively moved through love. I am naturally and instinctively moved through faith, optimism, and gratitude.

With some people, their emotion is tied to their

circumstances. If they've got money, they're happy. If they don't have any money, then they're deeply unhappy. Their mood and relationship with others are affected by this outside source. That's why, in your environment, in order for you to really manage your emotion, you've got to manage who you let into your life right now. Who are you allowing into your energy space right now? Because it's impacting your surroundings and your environment, and it will ultimately impact your desired outcome.

You've got to start paying attention to the energy of the people that are around you. I pay attention to some of the most minute things about people, and I encourage you to start doing the same. Pay attention to someone's tonality when they speak. What inferences can be made by their tone? I pay attention to their speaking volume. Do they seem to talk over everyone? Are they quiet? I pay attention to body language. I notice if someone seems apprehensive or closed off. If you are going to work with me—if you are going to be around me—when you get with me it must be 100%. It absolutely has to be 100%! You've got to come in with the right energy. If I'm allowing you into my world, I'm allowing you into this environment I've curated for myself that produces my success.

It may seem defensive of me, but that's the way you've got to be. In order for you to flourish, it has everything to do with being in a favorable environment. So most definitely, I take action to protect my favorable environment and you should do the same. Try it today with anyone you know that is in your environment. Watch their body language, listen to their tone. Does it match the favorable environment you need for your success? Does it bring you down? Check your own emotions and determine how you're being affected by it and be mindful of the emotions you experience when you're flourishing. Your goal is to maintain that emotional state of flourishing no matter what is actually going on around you and no matter who is talking.

Another aspect to creating this thriving environment is having the visual picture. I've always benefited from having imagery of the end goal I desire surround me. I've got to have the sign. I've got to have the words up. I've got to be downloading the right information. I download it by having it in my given environment at all times. It subconsciously enters my mind and becomes a part of my conscious reality.

I didn't grow up with a silver spoon in my mouth. My family was doing well in Nigeria for all intents and purposes. I spent ten years of my life there. My dad played professional tennis and my mom was an entrepreneur. They both worked really, really hard to give us a decent life. But when we came here to the States, my mom, myself and my two sisters were on welfare. We were on food stamps. This was before food stamps were loaded onto a debit card for you, so checking out in the grocery store took far longer, as the clerk would have to check each food stamp for an item. At least with a debit card, you keep some of your dignity when you checkout. With the old food stamps, everyone in line knew you were using them.

I recall my mom having to use food stamps for cash. Ten dollars' worth of food stamps was equal to five dollars in cash. Twenty dollars was equivalent to ten dollars. I remember those amounts so vividly.

I remember the first car my mom bought. It was a 1979 Pontiac Coup deVille. We even named the car—Mercy—because it was by the mercy of God that we could travel to wherever we wanted to go in it. This was part of my everyday reality, yet I did not let that define me by reliving those feelings and continuing to dwell on that part of my past as if it is part of my present.

Based on my youth and most circumstances of life, I'm not supposed to be a multi-millionaire. I'm not supposed to be a billionaire. I'm not supposed to be successful, because it wasn't something that was even considered a possibility when I was growing up. It wasn't a part of the visual or mental environment that was around me as a kid. But I learned the information I'm giving you. I learned how to create the right environment and the right conditions so I could flourish. Those conditions are just as much mental as they are physical.

Ask yourself what you want. Think about the end result you wish to obtain for yourself. If it's $10,000 per month, then print that out. Put it everywhere. Stick it on the refrigerator in the kitchen. Tape it onto your bathroom mirror. Place it by your bed. Stick it on your dashboard in your car. Make sure it can be seen everywhere you look. What you are doing by making sure you can see "I earn $10,000 a month" all over your house and in your car is creating the proper conditions for that to actually happen. You're creating the right surroundings and you're allowing your subconscious mind—the part of your mind that doesn't judge and is always aware—to believe you make that money, and that it is already a part of your reality.

Even throughout our toughest times, my mom still read self-help books, and that literature became a part of our surroundings. Having that reading material available to me, and understanding how those lessons would allow me to achieve exactly what I desired in life, were important steps in my pathway to perfecting my surroundings.

In our session, I will ask you to look around you right now. You can do this as you're reading this book. What are your surroundings? Your surroundings are what you see. Look it up in the dictionary, what does *surroundings* mean? "The things or conditions around a person or thing."

What are the things around you? If those surroundings are favorable, you're going to flourish, ladies and gentlemen. You're going to flourish and thrive! Therefore, you absolutely have to take control over what, and who, is around you, and thus you will be able to manage your emotions and your path forward.

I want you to develop two extremely powerful emotions: love and gratitude. In order for you to thrive right now, instead of survive, you absolutely must *show* and *feel* **love** and **gratitude**.

You've got to be able to proclaim, "I'm grateful!" at any given time. You need to be able to say, "I'm grateful for what happened today, whatever the technical difficulty was." Being able to show gratitude puts you in a state of already having that which you desire.

"I'm so grateful for my $10,000 per month income!"

You have to reach the actual, real emotional state you would be in if you already had the $10,000 per month income. How would your gratitude feel if you already had it? Would you also be grateful that you didn't have to worry about paying bills? Would you also have gratitude for the other ways your life improved by having a larger income? Feel gratitude for every bit of it all, as though you already possess those things.

If showing gratitude and love for something you don't already have is a difficult concept, practice the emotions of gratitude and love toward something you feel comfortable with already having. Let's say you go out and eat at your favorite restaurant. You sit down at the table, order your favorite dish, and it is served to you with perfection. Before you begin eating it, say to yourself, "I'm so grateful for this meal, it's my favorite. I absolutely love everything about it and I'm so grateful I am here enjoying it." By doing this, you're putting yourself in the environment of already having the thing you desire—which is your favorite meal. You can smell the atmosphere, you can feel the comfort of knowing you *have* the meal, you *already possess it*. After you leave the restaurant, you can recall the gratitude for the meal, the way the restaurant looked and smelled, and the way you felt while you were there enjoying your desired object.

Practice this same theory of showing emotional love

and gratitude with something you want to be your end result. If it is an amount of money, practice gratitude for seeing your bank statement reflect those earnings. Feel the emotion of gratitude—just as you would have for your favorite meal—for your desired outcome. You are so *grateful* that you are making that comfortable amount of money. Feel it! Replace any thoughts or feelings of lack of your desired goal with gratitude for already having it—even if you have not yet attained it. You're creating the right environment for it to exist by giving energy through your gratitude for having it.

The key, as with anything, is to be able to visualize it in your mind and maintain the emotion.

Once you've practiced gratitude for your desired outcome, ask yourself how you might be able to go around sharing love right now. Who can you encourage? Who can you help? Who can you give to? The proof of love is giving. It can be in the form of the giving of resources or the giving of time or of energy. Not everything you give has to be material. If you need proof of that, it's very simple. "God so loved the world that he gave his only begotten son" (John 3:16). Giving comes after the love. If you say that you love, then give. Gratitude goes along naturally with love. You show these things with your words and you show these things with your deeds.

Practice showing love when it feels like you normally wouldn't or couldn't. You can begin practicing this by giving love to something you normally take for granted. Start small in order to understand the simple mechanics of giving love. "I love my friend's enthusiasm. I'm so grateful I have them to talk to." "I love that I get to use this microwave oven, it makes heating up food so easy!" What can you add to your list of giving love to?

One of the most essential points when showing gratitude and love is to maintain it, regardless of the circumstances. There is always a reason for someone to make the excuse that they can't be grateful or can't show love, but that simply won't get you anywhere. Whatever is going on in your life right now, good or bad, say, "God, I'm *grateful* for what's happening. I know there is something you are teaching me here. Show me what the lesson is. I'm grateful for the $10,000 per month. It may not be here right now, but I'm grateful for it!"

Let yourself be excited about what is to come as though you already have it—it's already happened to you! Let your inner voice say, "Boy. I'm so excited about this! This is what I'll be able to do for my family. This is what I did for myself."

Take pictures of the car you are going to drive or the home you are going to live in. Make them readily available to you. Print them and place them where you will see them. Every day, say to yourself, “I’m so happy and grateful now,” while thinking on the things you want to bring into your life.

Right now, in our world, we are dealing with a tremendous loss of life with everything that’s going on. In fact, this statement is often true regardless of the current events. There is always something that we can find to dwell on that would be the cause of our depression and woes. But ask yourself, “What can I do?” As I write this book, I am asking myself, “What can I do for you?” I want to give love and share these tools with you.

Think deeply on how you react and respond to the people in your life. How are you showing love to the people who are still here right now? How are you giving to those people so that when they do go, you don’t have the pain of regret? That is something I wish I had done a little bit more. I wish I had made that phone call. I wish I had spent more time with my mom. I wish I had spent more time with my dad. I wish I had spent more time with my sisters and brothers. It’s important to note that these feelings are real—they’re part of the human experience. Although I admit that I think of these wishes, I do not dwell on it or let these wishes define me. Instead,

I pay it forward by giving as much love and gratitude as I can to those who are in my life so that I'll never find myself wishing I had done more or given more.

Your next step in showing love and gratitude is filtering out the energy that does not belong in your environment. What words are you allowing into your ears? The words you hear are either giving you *life* or they are giving you *death*. It is your choice how you choose to filter them.

According to Scripture, faith is the "substance of things hoped for, the evidence of things not seen" (Hebrews 11:1). Do you have any evidence of what you cannot see? When you have faith, it means you have some evidence of what you can't see. You can't see the jet right now. You cannot see the million dollars a day right now. But you *do* have evidence. Your evidence is your faith. You have the substance of what you desire. You have the ability to feel the exact same emotions you will feel when you are experiencing your desired outcome. Remember, if you have evidence, then you have faith. I have evidence. I have evidence in my goals. The end result of the goal is the evidence you need in order to understand you have faith.

The dictionary definition of *faith* is "complete trust

or confidence in someone or something." Everything that is going on in your life right now is something you can practice being grateful for. Be grateful for the opportunity to develop faith. Say, "God, I'm grateful for the opportunity to develop faith."

My faith is much stronger today than when I first began, and it keeps growing. There is no half-way, no 25%, no in-between. If you think your goal is complete, you're not showing complete faith or confidence.

Do you put your faith into someone else besides yourself? Have you made the connection as to who that someone is? If that someone is Donald Trump, if that someone is the Republican party, or the Democratic party, or Barack Obama, or your momma, or your daddy then yes—you may have a problem. If you are putting your faith in others, if you are putting your faith in your job, if you are putting your faith in your business, if you are putting your faith in your pastor then you have a serious problem.

Personally, I have faith and trust in God. Even when I fall, I know he has got me. That is where your confidence cannot be shaken. I've seen too many Red Seas being parted for me to doubt God. So why shouldn't I be growing right now? Why shouldn't I be happy right now? Many times, people will sell themselves short of happiness right now, in this moment, because they are still in a mindset of, "It's coming. It hasn't happened yet, so I cannot be happy yet." However, when you have faith and trust in God, you understand that you can be happy *now* for the things you want.

You have every opportunity and every chance right now to develop the power of faith. What is it that you want? What is it that you desire? What is it that you must have right now? Write it down, speak it, create it, create the evidence and surroundings—pictures, signs, words, images, bring forth the right people. Create for yourself a natural, instinctive state deriving from circumstances, relationships, mood, or connections with others. Ask yourself who the people are that you need to have in your life. Who are the people you need to spend time with? Who are the people you need to call? Who are the people you need to text? Write their names down and make sure that your connection with them helps develop your environment and breeds your success.

When you ask yourself who it is that you need to spend time with, it creates a re-evaluation of where your energy is spent. This becomes critical because it is where your hope is going to come from. Are the people you are spending time with building you up? Are they speaking life? That is how you are going to thrive in this year and into the next one. This is how each year will scaffold off the one before and lead to unprecedented growth. By creating the right conditions and surroundings and creating the right environment, you are going to allow yourself to thrive versus to just merely survive.

LESSON THREE

FINDING EPIC COURAGE

Courage is the ability to contain your fear in a dangerous or difficult situation. If you can do this, there are so many gifts for you on the other side of your fear.

Repetition is the key to winning, and it is the secret every champion knows. This is especially necessary during these unknown times. It takes courage to continue practicing repetition when you feel the fear of uncertainty. If you are reading this, I want to congratulate you. Right now, maybe more than ever before in your life, it is critical that you make daily success habits a practice.

If you can do this—if you are committed to not allowing fear to run your life—then I promise you that you'll receive an abundant payoff. The work comes in continuing to make this decision. Show up and practice your daily success habits.

I have been called to reach as many people as possible and deliver another kind of message. There is enough of your own type of messaging going on out there. I want to offer you something else, a theme called "Epic Courage."

If you are going to survive you are going to need massive amounts of *courage*. Webster's dictionary defines courage as "the mental or moral strength to venture, persevere, and withstand danger, fear or difficulty."

Courage is not a way of being, it is not a natural state. It's a choice. Right now, you may be at a crossroads in your life. You may be faced with extreme uncertainty. Perhaps you lost your job or someone you know is ill. Maybe you're worried about not being paid on time. Maybe you are concerned you will not have clients for your business. Everyone on the planet is facing variations of the same fears.

Courage is about feeling the fears yet choosing to take action. The Book of Proverbs tells us that fear and courage are brothers, and courage requires you to follow your heart. I could have waited months or even a year to launch Believe Nation, but I knew it was needed now. I wasn't going to let any expert hold me back and tell me this couldn't work or work right now. Right now, this is the moment, as you are reading this. Since we have launched, thousands and thousands have made the decision to become citizens of Believe Nation.

Courage is facing adversity with gratitude and love, and not giving in to the negative emotions that will only bring you down. When you feel like giving in and things feel off, you have the choice to either dwell on those negative feelings or to replace them with gratitude for what you have and what is to come.

There is a lot to learn about courage. Courage is a

choice. It's a choice to get up and face the world with faith and hope and a winning attitude. Courage is choosing to lead instead of cower. Courage is about being willing to block out the noise to see new opportunities; to adjust and create a life of meaning, abundance, prosperity and joy.

You can do this right now. You are *one choice away*. When was your breakthrough moment? Where did your mind go when you thought about having courage in a tough situation? What really struck you within this topic of courage being necessary for you to thrive? I challenge you to go and inspire someone today with courage, as we're better together.

Here is a helpful thought exercise for shifting to a state of complete courage while manifesting your desire. After you have defined your desire and you fully choose to live in faith for your desire, construct an event that you believe you would encounter after your desire has actually come to pass in your reality. This event you think of has to imply you've gotten exactly what you want. For example, if your desire is to live in a specific house on a specific street, then you will mentally construct an event that takes place in that exact house. This is also why I keep reminding you how important it is to go to open houses, eat in the expensive restaurants, or to go sit in your dream car at a dealership. It makes this exercise that much more effective when you know what it feels like. Use people you know in this exercise to bolster the reality of your mentally-constructed event.

It is key for you to let yourself become perfectly still and relaxed. Your physical body should feel calm and you should feel comfortable enough to drift off to sleep—but you don't actually want to go to sleep. Next, with your body calm and your eyes closed, you will use your physical senses to feel yourself right into the scene you've constructed.

You are creating a scene in the present moment in your mind. Using the desired house as our example, you're going to feel everything in that house presently.

A full mental construct with action and use of your senses might come in the form of hosting a housewarming party at your new dream house. You see your actual friends and family in the house, admiring the interior design, using the sink in the kitchen. One of your guests comes up to you and asks you where the bathroom is. You happily direct them to it, motioning down the hallway with your hand. You hear how the front door sounds when it opens and closes. You smell the fragrance of catering and candles. You sit on the sofa in that living room and experience the sensation of your knees bending slowly as you lower yourself to it and begin to sink into the comfort of the material it is made of. Someone you know quite well walks up to you and congratulates you on your amazing home. You can hear their voice with perfect clarity, as though it is recorded in your mind, and you thank them.

The importance of getting into a calm, relaxed state helps you focus on the direction of your thoughts without distractions. You are still able to be attentive to all of your mental constructs without outside efforts. What you are essentially doing is making the future part of your present reality—your *now*.

It will take your courage to practice this because you cannot let fear stop you. You have to have the courage to fully immerse yourself in your mental event. It's next-level visualization. You're not just visualizing yourself in action as though you are watching yourself in a movie. You need to see the entire event you've created in the first person. Once you practice this, you'll appreciate the difference it makes.

When I first began practicing visualization like this, I got out all the pictures I had taken of myself in the car I wanted to drive, or in the house I wanted to buy, and I studied them to put myself back into the environment of existing in them. I had *experienced* the environment I wanted as my everyday reality, so I would sit and construct an entire event happening inside those environments. It's important to note that I also imagined this from my first-person perspective and not like I was watching myself on a screen.

During this practice, if your attention does wander off, bring it back to its task by doing a repetitive action in your mind within your mentally constructed event. If it's at your housewarming party, make it an action like walking into the kitchen and opening the oven. Do it over and over again and continue doing it until the action has all the sensations of what it really feels like to do that action. Keep it in first person. Keep conjuring up what you smell, what you taste, what you hear, what you feel and what you see from your perspective. You might feel yourself getting mentally exhausted and tired during this exercise, especially when you're already in a relaxed state of mind. That's okay, you can still control your mental actions even if you're drowsy.

Remember, you've got to maintain courage in understanding that time is a man-made construct and distance is relative. In fully practicing your belief and visualizing at this level, involving all of your senses, you can take yourself hundreds, if not thousands, of miles away from your objective in point of space and years away in point of time. Don't get caught up thinking that those are obstacles you have to stay attached to. Detach yourself from that type of thinking and do it with full faith and courage.

LESSON FOUR

FAITH DURING UNCERTAINTY

You've been reading about thriving during difficult times. No doubt, you've picked up on the fact that it's about making a decision to lead, win, and create the results you want in your life no matter what. Now, I want to examine your faith.

Currently in our world, we have entered into an unprecedented time—a period of unknown territory. We're breaking new ground, and what you are going through right now—what we are all collectively going through right now—is going to require more faith than you've ever had before.

It's important to understand that faith is your lifeline. Faith is what is given to you by God. It does not operate based on what you see with your eyes. It goes beyond what you can physically see. Faith is actually about what you are hearing. Hearing is more important than actually seeing. It affects your inner thoughts and dialogue.

What you hear also creates imagery in your mind, so when you hear something, you envision it in your mind's eye and relate to it with your given experiences.

The opposite of faith is fear and doubt. Doubt is activated when you operate with only what you can see in the tangible world. My question to you is this: with the global crisis happening right now in the world, have you turned to faith? Or have you turned to doubt? Are you relying on the natural things you can see in the news headlines? Are you hanging on to the total amount of money in your bank account? Are you making decisions and taking action—or no action—based on what you can see with your eyes? Or are you operating from a place beyond the doubt into the unseen? Are you operating in faith right now?

There is a verse from Hebrews that says that "faith is the substance of things hoped for and the evidence of things unseen" (Hebrews 11:1). What do you desire that you are not seeing in your life in this very moment? Are you believing what you can see, or do you have faith in the unseen? Do you have faith that everything will work out? Faith that, despite the circumstances, you are being watched over and that you can create the life of your dreams?

Equate faith with planting a seed. Once the seed has been placed in the ground and covered with dirt, you have faith that it will grow. You know what the end result will look like. You don't go and dig the seed up every day to see if it has sprouted or how far along it has come—that will destroy it! You have faith in the process. It is that same faith you should apply to your dreams.

I have one last critical piece about faith to share with

you: "Faith without works is dead" (James 2:20). This means that you must show up in your life and take action. You can't sit around and hope and wish everything will blow over and that you'll be okay. It means you must get up and take action right now. You must take action as an act of faith in your life. It means showing up with a Plan A because there is no Plan B.

What does showing up look like? If your dream had been to become a player in the NBA, you wouldn't have just wished for it to happen. You would have to show up—meaning you would have to go practice, join a team, and demonstrate the action of making effort. If you're waiting for your dreams to happen to you instead of going out there and taking action to ensure they will, then your perfect desires aren't going to come true.

Claim your faith and post your most exciting and inspiring breakthrough moment today in Believe Nation. And remember *all things*—not small things—are possible if you believe (Mark 9:23).

LESSON FIVE
SEEING OPPORTUNITIES

An important daily success habit to help you thrive in your life is learning how to recognize your opportunities. This is a critical skill to creating movement in your life right now when so many other people are stuck and afraid. I'm sure you've heard the saying, "How you do one thing is how you do everything." My question for you is this: how are you going to handle this challenge? Who are you going to become during this global crisis? Are you going to come from a place of fear? Because from that place and from those lenses you'll only see more proof of why you should be afraid.

What you think about will expand and grow; your life follows your thoughts. Therefore, if you are afraid and have made no attempt to transform your fears into faith, you will foster the growth of fear and take actions that support you being afraid. You're going to end up with a result that's based on fear and surviving, not thriving.

What if you could turn crisis into opportunity? What if you could start today with seeing the world—even in its current state—as an opportunity to do better things? What if you could do more for your purpose in this world right now? This world is starving for leadership. You can make a difference in the lives of people around you. I want you to take this daily success habit of seeing challenges as opportunities and make them real. Don't just do this one day, do it every day. Ask yourself, "Where's the good in this situation?" Find the opportunity to show up and serve.

Guess what? Obstacles are going to come up again and again. Life does happen. It's usually not on the scale of a global pandemic, but I'm choosing to view this situation as it being bigger than the crisis. The bigger the opportunity, the bigger the reward. I want to charge you with *leveling-up* your leadership skills. Look for goodness and look for the opportunity to move in the direction of your dreams. Use Believe Nation and share with us what opportunities you see in order to make a real difference in the lives of others, toward your goals, and Believe Nation.

An important component to being able to recognize opportunities is being able to understand what your reality is and what reality actually *means*.

Your consciousness is the only reality.

That's what I mean when I talk about conceiving. What you conceive—the thoughts you picture and hear in your mind—comes from what you perceive, which is derived from your senses. That makes up your waking consciousness, which is what you feel as being awake and aware of your surroundings. No one can see your reality for you; you're the only one experiencing it—therefore, it simply is the only reality.

In the Old Testament, you will discover many allegories and stories that actually have deep interpretations that explain your power of I Am and the true power of what it means to believe.

Before I give an example of one of those stories, I want to provide you with a little bit of history to understand the source of the words used in the text. Remember, words are powerful. Words make up belief. The ancient Hebraic language that the Old Testament was written in was not a common language that everyone used. It was a reverent language and the words were considered *ineffable*. Ineffable means "unable to be spoken." The words that made up the stories—even the name of God—were too extreme and powerful to be expressed verbally.

Think about that. Today, we say just about anything. We speak all the time and express ourselves through spoken words and texts constantly. Our ancestors had a deep respect for the power of words, so much so that something especially sacred to them was not to be uttered by just anyone.

Ancient people who understood their language wrote down names and phrases with symbols that weren't phonetic representations of words from the language.

They didn't use an alphabet that made sounds like ours does. Instead, they knew what each symbol fully represented just as modern scientists understand that complex equations are represented with a single symbol. Written language wasn't something they used to express their thoughts or beliefs like we do now with our modern languages. One of the most popular examples of this is the way they wrote God's name. It was extremely symbolic. The first letter, "JOD," in the name GOD is a symbol for "hand"—specifically the hand of a leader. If there is one human body part that distinguishes humans from other living creatures, it's our hands.

When you get what you desire, you no longer want it the same way. The urgency is removed. If the desire persists, you did not actually succeed in believing you are what you desire to be. There still existed some small notion of not being successful when you stopped your visualization and with the activities in your waking, conscious day.

If I can feel that I Am that, when but a few seconds ago I knew I was not, then I am no longer hungry for it (more on the I Am in Lesson 8). I am no longer thirsty because I feel satisfied in that state. Then something shrinks within me, not physically but in my feeling, in my consciousness, for that is the creativeness of man. He so shrinks in desire, he loses the desire to continue in this meditation. He does not halt physically; he simply has no desire to continue the meditative act. "When you pray, believe that you have received, and you shall receive" (Mark 11:24). When the physical creative act is completed, the strength which is upon the hollow of man's thigh shrinks, we find ourselves weakened. In like manner, when someone believes successfully, they believe that they already have what they desire. What this does to the mind in terms of belief is it halts the active desire to obtain success. You can't long for and desire what you already have!

This feeling of already having your success, and knowing it just as confidently as you know the sun sets in the west, has to be physical with psychological feelings.

When you've successfully *believed* in your goal, you'll actually open up your reality to opportunities you didn't realize you had before. Have you ever experienced what happens when someone you know and think about often gets a new car, and the model and the color are unique? Suddenly, because this person you care about and hope to see is imprinted onto your subconscious mind, you will notice that exact type of car—even down to the same color—everywhere! It seems like it serves no purpose for this to happen other than making you think of the person consciously. But what it really does is it activates our human ability to empower our subconscious to see things that we need to see to be successful. It only seems like a futile effect because, over time, we've experienced the effect in such a simple way. What you've got to understand and believe is that you can cause the same effect to happen—but instead of seeing identical cars, you'll see opportunities, meet people, and come across new knowledge and material you didn't have before.

If one of your desires is to have more opportunities and have them become more obvious to you, you have to realize you can't make that your reality by paying for it from the material world.

You have to take on the belief that you're secure that opportunities are yours. It is a conscious knowing. Yes, you are supposed to immerse yourself in the environment of your desires—sit in the car, visit the house, wear the clothes—but just continuing to look at successful people and materializations of wealth will not get you where you want to be. You have to make your desires part of your conscious awareness. When you go for a walk, consciously realize you already are the wealthy person you desire to be. From that conscious activity, opportunities will begin to present themselves. It is like you are turning your radio dial into the station of your successful self.

I am fully conscious of being what I do not want to be. But knowing this law by which a man transforms himself, I assume that I am what I want to be and walk in the assumption that it is done. In becoming it, the old man dies and all that was related to that former concept of the self dies with it. You cannot take any part of the old man into the new man. You cannot put new wine in old bottles or new patches on old garments. You must be a new being completely. As you assume that you are what you want to be, you do not need the assistance of another to make it so. Neither do you need the assistance of anyone to bury the old man for you.

"Let the dead bury the dead" (Luke 9:60). Do not even look back, for no man having put his hand to the plow and then looking back is fit for the kingdom of heaven (Luke 9:62). Do not ask yourself how this thing is going to be. It does not matter if your reason denies it. It does not matter if all the world round about you denies it. You do not have to bury the old. You will bury the past by remaining faithful to your new concept of Self, and you will defy the whole vast future to find where you buried it.

The reason I shared these biblical stories with you is because you can allegorically apply their lessons to every day of your life. From interpreting them and knowing how sacred the language—the actual words—were to them, you can understand that our ancient ancestors fundamentally had the same need for success and achieving goals as we do now. We just have different views on what success is because of the society in which we live.

The hunt for opportunity has always existed and been an ever-present desire for humans, so we can learn from lessons of our ancestors in how to truly believe and achieve our dreams from these stories from humanity. If the clothes you are wearing now do not fit who you want to be—who you are in the future—then by the power of your imagination and belief, visualize yourself as what you want to be, wearing the clothes that the successful you must wear.

Do this with every aspect of your desired self.

PART TWO

LESSON SIX

IDENTIFYING YOUR LIMITING BELIEFS

STEP I

Take inventory of your limiting beliefs. In order to do this correctly, you must consider all of the current situations in your present life and assess them. Simply put, taking inventory of yourself is nothing more than a self-evaluation. Most of the time, we think of self-evaluation in terms of the physical—what we can see in the mirror. That is part of it, but you have to be able to reflect on how you think, how you feel, how the situations in your life make you feel and how you react to them, and how you believe you make other people around you feel. This can be challenging for people who may not have ever been asked to do this before. It can be hard to face aspects of yourself that aren't so positive. But in order to create change and identify the things that are holding you back, taking inventory of your limiting beliefs and understanding the source of them must be done.

One of the biggest hurdles in identifying your limiting beliefs is noticing something you've taken to be a truth in your life and peeling back the layers to discover it was never a truth at all; rather, it was something implanted in you from things that were said to you or things you heard. These false truths can be difficult because they have become hardwired into your psyche. It takes your mental fortitude to be brave and identify it, call it out for what it is, and label it as something that limits you.

STEP 2

I want you to say or do the complete opposite of whatever the limiting beliefs you identified are. You may have identified just one limiting belief, or several. They could vary from area to area in your life. If you had a limiting belief about your finances, then you must develop a belief that states the exact opposite of that belief. If your original belief was, "My family has never had wealth so I probably won't make it to be a millionaire," you must change that to say, "My family's history with money doesn't matter. I am a millionaire." If someone told you that you'll never amount to anything in your life, you would reverse that into a statement like, "I am living out my goals and dreams and there is so much more to come for me!"

I want you to decide to make a decision on what empowering beliefs you want for your life. Your empowering belief must be the complete opposite of the limiting beliefs that you know you've had. You cannot develop the opposite version of the limiting beliefs you were given until you completely identify what those limiting beliefs are, so if you feel there might be more under the surface, go back to step one and reassess what thought patterns and ingrained beliefs are holding you back. What are those things that you've said to yourself that have held you back? What have other people said to you over and over and over again that you have now accepted as truth?

STEP 3

In the difficult times in which we live, many people have been dealing with health issues. It is clearly a very challenging time for many people in our world. However, the truth of the matter is it has *always* been challenging. The past five years have been challenging. The last ten years or even the last one hundred years have been extremely difficult. Think back on your middle school history lessons. In the last hundred years, people survived illnesses that used to decimate populations and leave people scarred or crippled for life. Now, we have greater medical technology and more advanced research. They didn't have those things hundreds of years ago. We have access to information, medical care, vaccines and other life-saving aspects of modern medicine. We can Google our symptoms when we feel sick. We can go to the pharmacy and find remedies. We can see a doctor over a video call so that we don't have to leave our home to receive a medical evaluation. Are these times challenging for us? Yes. We have no other lifetime experience with which to compare it. We can only know what we can experience. But know that life is always challenging—for everyone and in a myriad of ways—regardless of the time period.

I want you to make the decision that regardless of

what's going on, you are going to be in a state of belief. Why not live the way you want to live before it turns around? Why wait?

Look at the word: *Be-lief.*

It actually means "to be glad and to be happy."

I can create a statement about any particular situation and use it, and now I can actually live happily. Even if what is going on around me is not great, I can mentally live in a state of happiness. You should be excited that you don't have to wait for it to show up in the physical in order to actually be glad and for you to experience happiness. That's what it means to be in a state of belief—to be happy.

If you have an empowering belief and you are claiming your rights, then you have control over your life, and you have created a statement. Decide what it is that you want. What type of life do you want? How do you want to operate within your faith?

After you've examined your former, false beliefs and developed new beliefs, ask yourself how you want to operate within your family. How do you want to operate within your family when it comes to your finances? How do you want to live when it comes to your fitness and your health?

Create specific, tailored, empowering statements for each one of the aforementioned areas of your life. A statement that I've used for many, many years is, "I'm so happy and grateful now." This statement blankets any situation with gratitude, and it puts the statement into this moment of now—not tomorrow or later—now, presently.

One of the biggest effects you may have on your family is what you speak over them. Are you speaking life over your family? Are you the person that is determining through your words the generational wealth you are creating for your family? I'm not just talking about your generational wealth in finance, I'm talking about legacy wealth. I want you to create a statement about every area—or any area—you want to focus on right now. "I am so happy and grateful now that..." That is the stem I want you to use to create an empowering statement.

When you create this statement, write it down. Put it in plain sight. You've got to be able to see your statement all the time, even in moments that you're not actively thinking about it. This is going to lead into step four.

STEP 4

I want you to *internalize* it. I want you to internalize

what this empowering statement you wrote is. The only way you can internalize something is through *auto-suggestion* and *visualization.*

Every single day, I want you to utilize the power of auto-suggestion. You need to repeat your empowering statement or belief about whatever area of your life to yourself—whether it's your faith, your family, your finances or your fitness—or all four areas. I want you to repeat it to yourself out loud at least ten times a day. Laugh to yourself through the day at least ten times a day. Say to yourself, "I'm so happy that I earn a million dollars a day." Then by implementing step four, through auto suggestion and visualization, this is your internalizing.

One of the biggest dangers of limiting beliefs is that they are internalized from an early age and often visualized without much effort. They became internalized from what you saw in your household, what you saw on TV, what you saw in your community and in your country. All of the actions that took place in order to internalize limiting beliefs must take place with your new beliefs in order to replace the old, limiting ones.

In order to internalize your new beliefs, you have to inundate your mind with where you want to go. Your mind is like a GPS device, and you've got to plug in the direction for where you want to go. Empower your mind to give yourself control and claim your rights. It is your right to be wealthy. It is your right to live an abundant life. It is your right to have love. It is your right to be happy.

Happiness is found within. That statement has so much faith in it because so many people around the world have been utilizing that statement. Happiness is not found in outward material things. Sure, material things can be really nice, but ultimately happiness really comes from within. The only thing that you produce from within is your energy and the words that are coming out of your mouth—your words are a form of your inner energy you're releasing. That's why I love the affirmations I learned from Bob Proctor.

When you apply step four and you internalize this information, you're going to build your faith up around whatever that goal is that you internalize through autosuggestion and visualization. What is faith? Faith is to have trust, to have confidence. Now, you have faith in God, you have faith in what you believe in. Imagine having faith in *yourself*. Imagine having faith in your own words. Imagine that! Faith is a muscle. It's got to be worked. You've got to be in the faith gym. How often are you coming to the faith gym? Step four is the faith gym. You must internalize your belief with your faith. Internalize the information. Regardless of whatever is taking place, there is always a way to get what you want.

Don't let yourself think or say that what you want is impossible. Do you want it? You do not have to use your moral code to realize it. It is altogether outside the reach of your code. Consciousness is the one and only reality. Therefore, we must form the object of our desire out of our own consciousness. People have a habit of slighting the importance of simple things, the suggestion to create a state akin to sleep in order to reach a fluid state, is one of the simple things you might slight. However, this simple formula for changing the future, which was discovered by the ancient teachers and given to us in the Bible, can be proved by all.

Belief is made real to us by experience. If you're not giving yourself a sensory experience of what it is you want, you can't imagine what it will be like to have what you desire. You will be out of your comfort zone and believe you don't belong within the environment of your desired state.

Remember, the you that you are at this very moment is the you that you have believed yourself to be.

Another way to describe belief is with the word *assumption*. Assumptions are beliefs and they create your reality. If you choose to assume everything always works out in your favor, then your reality will reflect that.

If you believe in any way right now that because you aren't physically seeing or experiencing things you desire, your visualizations and positive statements about yourself aren't truly working, then you must immediately limit that belief. You have to switch mental gears and speak about your belief with affirmations like, "I know I am successful. It doesn't matter what I used to think or what that person said to me, I *know*! I am a creator for my reality and I've created this great situation." You can make your own statements in a similar vein as these to realign your belief with your desire.

To truly believe and maintain your belief, you'll stop making limiting statements like, "It's on its way," or "It's coming." Those statements build the outcome of your reality into a state of constant waiting for your desires to arrive.

I don't believe that some people have the ability of belief and some don't. Everyone is born with the capabilities to believe, but not everyone is able to develop their belief skills. If you take the time to practice believing and implement these tools into your life, you will see your desired outcome.

Disbelief in your ability to have your desire, and being attached to the feeling of not having it, is the source of any failure you perceive.

LESSON SEVEN

CONTROLLING YOUR ENVIRONMENT DURING TOUGH TIMES

Fear is like a monster in that it is always waiting in the background for you to come find it. I want you to be careful not to feed that monster. You must shut it out. For me, that looks like not turning on the news or searching for the latest COVID-19 stats or updates or obsessing about it. I'm not going to prepare for anything but my future life. You've got to keep your eye on the prize and protect your heart, mind, and soul from fear that could lead you down the wrong path in the present moment.

Today's success habit is about creating a winning environment while the world around you is scared. In fact, you can't truly thrive without learning this and having incredible discipline around it.

Although most of the world right now is quarantined or in some form of shelter-in-place restriction, in the midst of all of this, there are opportunities. You cannot see them if you are not protecting your environment.

I want you to recommit yourself right now, today, to protecting your brain from allowing anything but positivity. Only positive messages should be coming into your life right now. Don't turn on the news; instead, fill your brain with books. Listen to audios like *Think and Grow Rich*, *The Magic of Believing* or *Conceive, Believe, Achieve*. There is an enormous variety of spiritual books that will increase your faith. If you have time for social media or listening to music in the car, then you have time to hold a book or play an audiobook instead.

Become more aware of sources of fear and negativity. Change the subject when others want to bring fear to you in their conversation. Respond with faith and love and *be* in faith and love. Be the encouragement for others, but let it start deep inside of you. There is not a single room I enter within my house that does not have some visual reminder of my goal. I hang up signs. I frame photos of where it is that I'm going. I put these visual triggers all over my house to help me protect my environment and create one that helps me win. In our exclusive Believe Nation community, I want you to tell me three adjustments you are going to make to your environment today to support you in the highest way possible. At this very time every single human on the planet is experiencing something challenging, and it's going to take courage — there is no doubt about that. I absolutely believe in you!

As your mentor, I'm not just here to inspire you. I want to inspire you into action. I want you to understand the meaning of **brave action for traction**. Right now, your actions need to be bold and they need to be brave. Revisit your personal success goal—that one thing you are so committed to creating in your present, waking life. I want you to ask yourself, "What brave action can I take in the direction of my dreams right in this moment?"

It does not matter what circumstance you are in right now; do not dwell on what you perceive as your present reality. Let that drift from your mind. Then I want you to ask yourself, "What am I afraid to do right now?" Identify why you are afraid to take brave action. Know what you need to do. Then you can ask yourself, "Where do I require more faith?"

Repeat after me right now: "I commit to facing the fears that are holding me back from greatness." I want you to repeat that again. Ask yourself what committing to facing your fears looks like to you. This is personal. What fears hold you back may not be even close to the same for your neighbor or your friend.

I'm still showing up every day, despite that experts told me not to, that it wouldn't work. Sure, I had to change my strategy a bit. But I'm holding to the course... no matter what. That's an example of the faith that is necessary to succeed. Therefore, if you're gaining from being a citizen of Believe Nation in any way, please help me spread the word.

Daily habits are imperative to regulating your intake of fear and negativity. You have to work at making your daily habits stick. Your daily habits are some of the most important facets of Believe Nation. Your innate ability to believe is one of the most important aspects of your life.

I truly believe that a person who learns how to believe will live a completely different life than those who either never learn to or who choose not to try and learn. Those who believe live lives that are more fulfilled.

Believers live with more joy and happiness. They live *within* the word believe. You are going to learn that within belief exists the definition of why you want to be a part of what we do at Believe Nation every single day.

From my experience throughout the last sixteen years that I have been an entrepreneur, I can tell you that daily success habits are exactly how I have gotten to where I am. If you talk to someone who has ever been successful at anything—sports, entertainment, business, family, faith—whatever it is, they are successful because they have actually developed the discipline of doing certain things every single day. They don't make excuses for days they couldn't do it. They do not waver. They find a way to make it happen for them every day regardless of any outside circumstances.

Compound what successful people do with what you see all around the world. When you watch someone operating at a very high level, it's not what they did one day, one week, or one month. It's what they did every day, every week, every month, and every year for many years. That's the price that you want to pay. What price will you need to pay?

If you look at social media—meaning you scroll through social media every single day (Facebook, Instagram, or Snapchat)—you have formed a daily habit of the consumption of other people's energy through social media. You are also immersing yourself in a mental environment. What exactly are you feeding yourself every time you go on social media? Negativity? Outrage? Mindless jokes? What sort of information are you downloading every single day on social media? What are you downloading into your mind when you watch TV, YouTube videos, cable news or cable talk shows? Everything you watch, you take in. You consume it—even on a subconscious level. If you do that every day of every week all year long, then you've made that into quite a serious habit. What is it doing for you? What are you gaining from it? Do the successful people that you know seem to do that, too? The reason Believe Nation was created is for you to have a place to go in order to start downloading *empowering* beliefs. It is an opportunity for you to have access to content that will help you live the life that you want to live.

The purpose of Believe Nation is to create a nation of people who are possibility thinkers, and doers of the impossible. But there's always a price to pay—in this case, the price is going to be discipline. Discipline is going to take you from wasting your time on information that doesn't really help you to being really locked into success habits. That's why Believe Nation provides the content that it does. As of the writing of this book, we have twelve models on the Believe Nation platform and they are explained thoroughly within the content of this book.

You must do the exercises provided so that you can track your growth when it comes to your belief. Anything you track will grow. Like the analogy of the seed from Lesson Six, what you track is your seed. You plant it, have faith that it is in fact growing, and you'll reap the reward. The way the tracking exercise fits into your life is that it is going to give you exactly what it is that you need from a belief standpoint in order to go out and to live life the way you want to live. That is the purpose for it. That is why we created it.

Your end goal that you have written down and placed around you is a reflection of how you truly want to live. In our world, people often forget that they are born with the tools to live life the way they truly want to and obtain the things they desire from life. Our society has a way of making people believe they are trapped. Believe Nation's exercises are meant to help inspire you that naturally, you have the tools you need to break free and live the way you dream of living. In turn, your achievements will inspire those around you. People who consume your content on social media—who spend all day endlessly and mindlessly scrolling—will come across what you have done and become motivated by it.

Even if what is going on around me is not great, I can mentally live in a state of happiness.

LESSON EIGHT

EMPOWERING BELIEFS

The moment when everything changed for me was when I truly understood the power I held. It has made all the difference. It has given me a sense of peace, true happiness, because prior to it I had a lot of worry, I had a lot of fear. I had a lot of uncertainty. I really wasn't quite sure how things were going to pan out. But once I understood the power of I Am, everything completely changed for me.

Back in 2010, I was living in an apartment, a nice apartment over by the Galleria area in Houston, and I was listening to an audiobook, as I typically do every day to build my mind. I was listening to this audio and the gentleman on there was speaking about words, and about the spirit. And it just clicked for me. Everything just clicked.

You may know my story; I grew up in church and I was there eight days a week, so I was very familiar with the things of God. But I don't think that I really understood it. I'm not sure that I really made that connection until 2010. My life was literally a blur those days. I don't remember anything happening for nine days except for crying because I felt like I had failed God. I felt like I'd finally gotten the connection and really understood what I had seen growing up. This is something that regardless of what your faith is, you will get it and really understand it and really have that sense of peace and joy and happiness, as well as knowing that everything is actually working out for your own good.

In this life-changing audio, I kept hearing this word—Spirit. I keep hearing that over and over again. And then it hit me like a ton of bricks, ladies and gentlemen. I was literally in tears like a brand-new baby. After that moment, for nine days, I don't remember doing my business, I don't remember talking to anyone. It was just nine days of crying in this newfound realization. Those were the greatest nine days of my life.

There are three key factors in creating your most empowering beliefs. It starts with your words and then it moves into your mental images, your ability to visualize and then finally, it is crystallized in your emotional state that you are in. Remember, belief is you accepting a statement as truth.

This unshakable, empowering belief you are creating starts with the **power of words**. There are two particular words that I have in mind. These are the two most powerful words that have ever been created. As a matter of fact, these two words are the Creator Himself. They are the words **I Am**. Your belief system must start with these two words. That is the foundation: I Am. The foundation is God.

Regardless of what your religious beliefs are, you will agree with me that I Am is the foundation. Whether you believe in Jesus, Buddha or Allah—that's your own personal preference. Personally, I don't believe that anyone is right or anyone is wrong...I don't make it my business to judge others' religious belief systems. I simply know that I have my own beliefs and that's where I teach from. I know that if you make that same connection I made ten years ago, your life will never be the same again.

The power of I Am can be found in Exodus 3:14. When Moses asks what he should call Him, God states his name to Moses for the first time.

So when I say the power of I Am—I am referring to God. "Who shall I say sent me?"

"God said to Moses, 'I am who I am.' And He said, 'Say this to the people of Israel: 'I AM has sent me to you'" (Exodus 3:14-15). I Am is the power of God, I Am is the power of true belief and faith. I Am creates belief systems.

In his teachings on the power of I Am, Neville Goddard stated that "[...]wherever you are in this world, whatever you're doing, if you could only remember the name of God and call upon it, instantly you will be redeemed from whatever you are—if you call upon it—in another state." Goddard was referring specifically to I Am, as it evokes the power of God within you to fully realize your beliefs and desires.

I Am is the start of everything. It creates everything. It is *transformative*. It changes things. It transitions you from your old reality to your new, dream reality. It allows you to grow and it grows things around you. But take caution, as it can also destroy things as well. The empowering belief that you need to have that you are creating for yourself must start with I Am. The Scripture also states that "In the beginning was the word, and the word was with God, and the word was God" (John 1:1). There was one clear definition after another explaining what I Am really was about. It existed from the very beginning of time.

Whenever I say I am so happy and grateful, whenever I am invoking the power of creation, that is the true power of understanding I Am. It is what I Am does. Anything you state after I Am goes directly into creation mode. If you want a belief system when it comes to your family, finances, your business, your health, start it with the power of I Am. Make statements like, "I Am so happy and grateful now that I have a healthy and fit body. I Am so grateful that my finances are absolutely exploding right now."

What you are invoking with I Am is the power—the *ultimate* power—to fully step into the particular situation you desire. Without completely utilizing the power of I Am, you can't create all the things that you want. But you, plus the I Am, plus the universe will yield the *you-need-verse*! And in this you-need-verse, you will get what you need!

Verse is a set of words that have been put together that have a rhythm. *Verse* is, by design, still just a compilation of words. But let us look at uni. *Uni* means "one." So, take one verse and one God. That's what universe means. When I made this connection, I realized that everything that I want to create and destroy, everything that I want to grow and transform, starts with I Am.

Think deeply about the I Am that you are saying right now. If they are limiting beliefs like, "I'm broke, I'm sick, I'm stuck," then you are utilizing this creative force in the wrong way.

If anything you say *to* yourself—or *about* yourself to others—resembles the above examples, your I Am is destructive, not creative. A good point to remember is that destruction is often viewed as a form of creation and furthermore, scientifically speaking, energy cannot be created or destroyed—only transformed. That makes the I Am a double-edged sword. You can take the energy of the universe, wield your word sword, and either create the life you want or destroy your dreams. If you look at the concept of the word sword, the whole world was created through words. You can't spell the word "world" without "word" in it. There is so much evidence out there about how powerful words actually are. However, you have to be very conscientious of this power. You have to be very conscious of what it is that you are saying.

When I first began to understand the power of I Am, right away I became very conscious of what I was saying. I held my awareness over my words over and over again, replacing negative statements with positive ones, until it became an unconscious action. Now, I only speak right things. A negative situation may come up in my life, but I am going to speak the right things about it and about myself. There may be darkness, but I am going to speak I Am. I Am going to speak, "I Am so happy and grateful."

I encourage you to speak like this as well because what you really want isn't made up of tangible things. It's not the money, the home or bank account. It's not success—that's not what you want. What you *really* want is the feeling of being happy, being loved and being grateful. Fundamentally, those are the things all of humanity strives to attain. Our society just makes it so that we associate the aforementioned material things with the emotions of happiness, love and gratitude—but those things aren't actually defined by anything material.

There are people who are grateful that they make $100,000 a year. There are people who are ungrateful that they make $100,000 *a month*. That's why I remind people to not be frustrated with where they are right now. If you don't learn to be happy and grateful in the present moment, where you are *right now*, then I believe that when you get to that thing that you believe is going to transform your life—when you get to that level of income where you think everything is going to be great—you are still are going to be frustrated and unhappy because there is always something more.

As humans, we are wired to want more. It's natural within us. That is God. God always wants more. He said, if you don't worship me, I'll have the rocks do it (Luke 19:40). That energy is what is inside of you. We all want more. The difference between a person who will achieve their desires and beliefs, and a person who will remain unhappy, is being able to be happy and grateful when you have not yet achieved your desired state. The notion that God has the ability to do all things—anything you want to create—is timeless. He's already done it. He has already done it in someone else's life, and it is already done in yours as well—your gratitude should match God's timing. If it's already done, then you should already show your happiness.

Genesis 1:27 states: "So God created mankind in His own image, in the image of God He created them; male and female He created them." This is further evidence of the power of I Am. God is the creator of all things, and we were made in God's image. Image doesn't just mean our physical appearance is like that of God; rather, it means we have attributes of God within us. We are all pieces of the same God—creator of the universe—and we were given the power of I Am to create the reality we perceive around us. That means each human who exists presently has this same power of creation. There's no rule saying every single person cannot have the success, wealth, or health in life that they desire. We have just set up constructs in society to make it seem like only a few people are entitled to our desires and our own personal definition of success.

Success looks different from person to person, from year to year, and from place to place. I set a goal to become a multi-millionaire and I achieved that desired targeted state using my I Am power. Someone else who lives in a completely different culture may have a personal goal that's not completely rooted in their finances. They still have the power of I Am within them and if they know how, they can use this power to achieve whatever their desire is.

Whatever it is that you want, He has already done

something greater. Because we think of things so linearly, it may be a difficult concept to imagine that all you desire *is already done*, but put your faith in the I Am, and know it has already happened for you. Think of how far humanity has come from day one. The same God that works in someone else works in you, too. The difference between you and that other person is the power of I Am. That needs to be your number one statement. You can't afford to speak the wrong words. You must speak the right words and those words start with I Am.

I watched Bob Proctor years ago on *The Secret*, and I have studied him over the years. He's someone I consider to be a coach...someone I actually listen to. He taught me the I Am affirmation. This introduction to the power of I Am transformed my thinking completely. This affirmation has literally transformed the lives of millions of people around the world—I Am so happy and grateful now. Create an I Am belief statement and let it start with I Am. It creates, it transforms...that's what it does.

The power of creation must be understood differently than preconceived notions you learned since childhood. When I tell you that by yourself, you can't do it, what I mean is without the power of I Am, you risk using wrong words, you risk letting doubt and negative beliefs seep in and poison your faith. But with I Am, nothing is impossible.

How does the I Am—God—see you? He doesn't see you as broke or average, nor does He see your shortcomings. That is what the enemy wants you to see... your shame and your guilt and your sins. I Am only looks at what you say after I Am. There is no weighing of your statement and no judgment of your empowering belief. I Am responds to your faith and your faith alone. You gain your faith from what you are hearing. Therefore, if all you are hearing is, "I Am so happy and grateful now!" then that is what I Am responds to—that's what God responds to.

Your faith will build and in the present moment, you begin to see yourself as healthy and wealthy. I saw myself as a rich man before I became rich. I saw it clear as day. I visualized who I am. I wrote it down. I put pictures up. I wanted to create an environment of a rich person. I didn't see the broke twenty-one-year-old. I saw the thirty-five-year-old David and the forty-year-old David. I'm not tied to a particular point in time. Even with all of the watches I own, none of them tell the same time anyway. Time is irrelevant to the I Am.

I am going to have my reticular activating system go to work for me. I am going to make it important by putting these images and pictures all around me so now when I go out, I only spot things that help me get what it is that I am believing for. Only the right people come into my life. Only the right circumstances present themselves. Inundate your life with the world you want to live in and you will see it reflected in your reality.

Take Kobe Bryant for example. Kobe *understood* the power of belief. Look at Michael Jordan. Michael also understood the power of belief, which is why there is a documentary about his six championships. He said, "I believed it." His use of the word *belief* encompasses everything I've asked you to practice. He had faith, he visualized his desired outcomes, and he was thankful for it in the present moment. We are still talking about him twenty-plus years later.

The power of I Am that I am sharing with you is meant to help you move past desire alone. By itself, just wanting something does not make change in your reality. Your belief and your desires are a force of nature that are not dependent on anything you have grown up thinking matters to achieve goals. Belief and desire have always existed, just like God existed before this universe. Put it into these terms: desire is an energy and your visualization is a template from which God, the I Am, constructs everything.

LESSON NINE

TRANSFORMING BELIEFS

You are going to transform your regular, everyday belief system into your present reality. You are going to begin to expand your belief system into an empowering, everyday belief system that gives you your present reality. You are going to demonstrate to yourself how to expand your regular belief system into an empowering belief system that shifts you into the direction of your goals and your dreams. You're going to create a specifically designed belief system to help you reach your goals. You're going to be able to see your own results.

Your senses might try and deny you fully experiencing the power of I Am at first. This is why you have to repeatedly affirm your I Am, and practice it using all of your physical senses in your imagination.

Experts estimate that the average person thinks between 60,000 and 80,000 thoughts a day. More importantly, about 95% of those thoughts are repetitive thoughts. Let that sink in for a moment.

Do you notice that you wake up thinking about the same things? These thoughts drive your actions. Your actions drive your results. What drives your results are your beliefs. Beliefs are both an incredible foundation and force, and they can move you in any direction--right or wrong. If you're going to naturally have repetitive thoughts all day, they need to be empowering ones.

Change your thought pattern from reflections of being stuck and lacking. Remember that you can't actually change your thoughts until you change your belief system. Going from normal belief systems to empowering belief systems is like upgrading your Honda Accord to a custom-made Rolls Royce. That's quite a big change. Empowering beliefs are about changing—going from limited thinking to limitless possibilities. Think about the results you are getting right now and the beliefs behind those results. What has driven your current results in your present reality? Don't dwell on it...but do take note of it.

Evidence of the power of your new belief system working will become apparent to you in your present reality. Your empowered belief system is like an FM radio station that you haven't tuned into before. You've been set on one frequency, listening to one station. That station has fed you negative thought patterns and trained you to not to be able to observe great opportunities or show gratitude for life. Once you turn that dial and tune into that new frequency, you'll shift everything you see, hear and experience. That will reveal itself in your tangible world.

When you inspire other people, you're giving them inspiring, positive energy. That inspirational energy will come back to you. This is not a mystical, karmic lesson.

It is the way giving works. If you give encouragement you are going to get encouragement. If you give belief to other people, you are going to receive belief. If you give money, you are going to get a lot of money back. Whatever you give, you get to keep. There is a hidden gift in your generosity, no matter what it is you're giving. The energy and emotion you put out into the world is always matched.

I can't stress the importance of the meaning of words enough. Take a look at the definition of the word empower.

em·pow·er
/əmˈpou(ə)r/

verb

1. give (someone) the authority or power to do something.
2. make (someone) stronger and more confident, especially in controlling their life and claiming their rights.

Empowerment is the ability to control our lives and to decide the direction that our lives are going. Oftentimes, people get caught up in the notion that there is no real control over where they are going in life, that a path has already been set forth, and they keep trudging along on it even though they're miserable. It does not have to be this way! It shouldn't be this way.

Look at your own life and the choices you think you have before you. Are you living an empowering life right now? Are you controlling your life? Are you controlling your birthright? It is about being aware of who *you* really are. So many of us are not aware of the power that's inside of us. Sure, you may have heard motivational speakers before tell you that you are in charge, or perhaps you have read a book on self-empowerment. But what did you do about it? What practices did you start doing daily that would help change your life? What actions did you take?

The reason why we don't live empowering lives is due to the lack of understanding that there is a choice, and you have autonomy over your own empowerment and environment. The idea that anyone else actually has control over how far you can go in life is an illusion.

LESSON TEN

TAKING INVENTORY OF YOUR BELIEFS

What do you believe about yourself? What do you believe is actually possible for you to achieve? Belief goes much deeper than a basic definition from the dictionary. Belief is seeing yourself with whatever it is you desire with your God-like eyes—your ability to visualize and see, with your mind's eye, exactly what it is you want to happen to you.

Belief is a very special word. It governs everything that happens in our world. It's a complex word because it represents such a deep meaning. When you're in a state of belief, you're affirming, "I'm loved by God," because of the etymology, or origin of the word belief. Belief allows you to live from the inside out. You're actually in control of what's happening to you, not what's happening in your outside environment.

You must learn to identify any beliefs you harbor about yourself that aren't true and create beliefs that actually reflect your desires for yourself and your life. Your belief has to be backed by your work—and your work is present in your activity and what environment you choose to exist in. You can do the same activity in a different environment and see change. It's like planting a seed. You can plant a seed just under the surface of some dirt on the ground and it won't grow. If you plant the seed in the right soil—the right environment—it will grow and flourish.

People who actually live empowering lives utilize four essential points in their creation of their own empowering beliefs. You must create your own personalized empowering belief and, in order to do so successfully, put forth energy in developing empowering beliefs in four key areas of your life.

You have empowering belief when it comes to your **faith**—whatever your faith is. Faith is individual to each person, so it's not about adhering to a strict dogma, it's about empowering what faith means to you.

You also want to create an empowering belief about your **family**. How do you think about your family? What does family mean to you, specifically? For many people, they view family traditionally. Other people may have grown up without a traditional mother and father and have a different take on family—however, family still exists to them in one way or another, so anyone can develop an empowering belief about family regardless of their personal circumstances. Dig deep within yourself and find out what it is that you believe about your family.

It is paramount that you have an empowering belief about your **finances**. Yes, money. Money is very, *very* important. What does an empowering belief about your finances look like to you? Write down statements that you find empowering about your finances. "Money comes to me easily. I don't struggle over my finances." That is an empowering statement that you can apply to your personal belief about your finances.

You need to have empowering beliefs about your **fitness** and your body. If you don't have the right energy, you are not going to go out there and do the work that is necessary for you to accomplish your goals. The fitness of your physical being is imperative because it is a reflection of your inner strength and focus. It maintains your physical being so that you can take action. Empowering your beliefs about your own fitness is also malleable in terms of how it applies to the individual. We are all different, so our best fitness and our most empowering beliefs about our fitness will vary from person to person. However, regardless of our individual differences, fitness is possible for each person. In terms of faith, you know what it means to you, individually, and you're going to need to move in that direction.

When it comes to your family, decide what role you are going to play. How is it that you operate within your family? What is it that you bring to the table when it comes to your family? If you are a provider for your family, they can't live without you. You already play that role. How can you enhance it? With regard to your finances, what empowering belief do you have? What are your goals and where are you going to be financially by the end of the year?

Another aspect of creating your empowering beliefs is your concept of where you are in time. Presently, you are where you are—but where are you going to be in the next five years? What about in the next ten years? Where are you going to be even further down the line? You can apply this concept of time to the four key points of creating empowering beliefs. Where are you going to be when it comes to your fitness? You need to make definitive answers to these questions for yourself. Take out the words "I might be" or "maybe" when answering these questions. You have to decide that you want to look a certain way and be a certain way. You want to have a certain vibration about your life—one that people can pick up on. You need a certain energy about your life. What are you going to eat? What are you not going to eat? What are you going to drink? What are you going to not drink? All of these aspects coagulate into your solid belief about yourself.

Lock down what your beliefs are about yourself in these four given areas. Take the standard definition of *belief:*

be·lief
/bəˈlēf/
noun

1. an acceptance that a statement is true or that something exists.
   "his **belief in** the value of hard work"

2. trust, faith, or confidence in someone or something.

To me, the most important word in that definition is "statement." A belief is a statement that you've accepted as true.

My next question to you is: what statements were said to you knowingly or unknowingly that you have accepted as truth? What beliefs do you have about yourself that were said to you when you were young that you didn't fully understand? What were things from your childhood that you thought your mind did not latch on to? That's the first step in order to recreate the empowering beliefs that you want to have. You've got to take inventory as to what statements, beliefs, and false beliefs have been given to you so that you may develop new, empowering beliefs that replace any untruths you've been given.

What was presented to you as a child? Were you brought up in an environment where there were many limiting beliefs? As a child, you may not have been capable of changing those limited beliefs. You did not understand what people around you were capable of doing. Now is the time to take inventory of all the beliefs given to you as a child because now, in adulthood, those beliefs are working either for you or against you. And how do you know that they are working for you? Just look closely at your life. Results never lie.

Take, for example, the small "facts" your parents may have told you as a kid. Let us say that you were told as a child that drinking lots of caffeine would stunt your growth. You may have avoided coffee until you turned twenty. Later, you found out that coffee has no adverse effects on growth and you realize your parents just didn't want a hyper kid running around. You then change your belief and when you have children, you may tell them something different about coffee. You may tell them that coffee will make them hyper and that it's more of an adult drink. They will then grow up with a belief about caffeine and coffee that has nothing to do with stunting growth whatsoever. Their environment and beliefs will be inherently different than yours were at their same age. This is also an example of the energy and emotions you give being matched. If you give truth in your beliefs to those you share them with, those truths will be reciprocated and in turn, the recipients of your beliefs will be motivated to spread the same type of beliefs as you have given them. There is a lot of power in that.

If you want to know whether your thoughts are empowering, look no further than your own beliefs and how they affect you and those around you. If you are on the right track, daily success habits are imperative for staying there. Now you are able to reinforce the right kinds of thoughts and the right kinds of beliefs over and over again.

You have to take inventory of your beliefs about yourself and about who you are. What were those limiting beliefs you once had? Make sure you identify all of them. Were you told growing up that you wouldn't amount to anything? That's a real, intrinsic belief for a lot of people who, unfortunately, were told that while growing up. Were you told that a certain, large amount of income was not meant for you? Some people were. Some people were told they were only expected to make the bare minimum to survive, and that belief has stuck with them. Were you told that you'll never have kids or you'll never be married? Is what you were told growing up still haunting you today? You've got to dig deep and really think about any beliefs you were given while you were growing up. Some beliefs aren't as obvious as the examples from above and could be hidden. You need to write down all the beliefs your family taught you to be true and carefully identify those that are limiting. You're the one that is going to need to be honest about all of this because you're the only one who knows what beliefs were given to you.

Once identified, whatever the belief is—what was told to you when you were growing up that you still believe today—make a note of it and work out how you can change it. For example, what are your beliefs about your health? Some people I've worked with have had family say things like, "Well, Aunt Marie gained weight after she got married and your mother did, too, so you can expect that you'll probably get big after you get married. It's in our family. It's just what happens," or, "Your grandfather had heart problems and so did your dad and uncles, so you probably will, too." Never mind that those family members may have never had any regard for diet and exercise...they planted the belief that heart trouble is inevitable.

I believe that if you can know the enemy, you can defeat the enemy. If you can identify what these limiting beliefs are and take inventory of them, then you can go about changing them.

LESSON ELEVEN
TRIANGLE OF BELIEF

Your belief system is made up of three things:

ONE

The words that you speak and hear;

TWO

The images that you look at;

THREE

The emotions created by the environment you put yourself in.

When you create an empowering belief, you make it true. Replace your limiting belief with an empowering belief that your brain believes is real. If you have a lingering thought in the back of your mind that reminds you of lack, that will sabotage your empowering belief.

LESSON TWELVE

FOUNDATION OF YOUR BELIEF

Faith is having complete confidence in someone or something. Faith is the belief in the unseen. You are going to need faith right now in order to create the future reality that you are not living presently. God, Source, Higher Power—you, the I Am in you, were created in God's image. The Spirit of God which created you resides *in* you. Claim that power—wake up to this and truly believe in yourself.

Faith is the belief in the unseen.

It's important to know where you are in this precise moment. I want you to take stock and inventory of where your belief system is at present. What current results are you getting in your life right now? What are you continuing to get in your life over and over? What thoughts are you aware of right now that you know you think of frequently?

LESSON THIRTEEN

MOVING FROM DISBELIEF

Both of my parents were actively engaged in our childhood. Their involvement in Christianity influenced our upbringing to include the basic concepts of belief and faith as a part of our daily conversations. They would talk to us often and involve themselves in our lives. But even though I was fully engulfed in concepts of belief and faith, I hadn't yet learned how to master my own belief or how to identify aspects of my belief system that didn't serve me.

How do you move from disbelief to unshakable knowing, or from doubt and worry to possibility?

You need to tap into the Higher Source. Belief as I am teaching it to you acts as a massive attractor—what you believe is what you bring into your life.

LESSON FOURTEEN

THAT MOMENT OF CHANGE

Nothing changes if *nothing* changes. It's important to learn to understand what hitting your own personal bottom looks like to you. For me, it looked like a lack of independence and of financial freedom. In 2009, I was broke. I lived with my father and slept on a twin-sized bed. I drove my mom's Chevy Malibu. When I was on business appointments, I would park that Malibu down the street, away from sight so that no one I was meeting with could see it. Once after an appointment meeting, I got into the Malibu and it wouldn't start. It took several minutes to get the engine going—I declared right then and there that I was done.

I was going to raise my standard. I was no longer going to live that way. I knew I was better than that. I went from being broke to earning six figures in six months. Eighteen months later, I was a millionaire. Your new life starts at an ending point. Creation is a form of destruction. I destroyed my old life and created a new one. Your "enough is enough" moment can push you to new levels. Don't hesitate to take a stand and make a change.

Is fear of failure keeping you from going to that next level? Take into consideration the difference between most champions and other people. They are aware of how much better they can be and are willing to work for it. They tackle their personal challenge with no fear. Kobe Bryant once said, "If you think you're going to fail, you probably will fail." Reaching that next dream—the car, house—what if you could change that belief in an instant? You've got to stay in the game. I can't take those steps for you; it must start with you. Repeat empowering beliefs over and over and retrain your mind.

Know that there is no average. Believe that you are more and that there is more for you. Most people think that they are not enough—that they are average. You may accept average, but you were not created to be average. To believe you are not good enough is to steal from your life. Believe that you are not average. The only way to not have regret is to go all out. Rise up to who you were meant to be. Take one giant step forward with a fear that may be holding you back. Don't walk away before the breakthrough happens.

You can tell what people believe about their own life by observing what they have brought into their life. You can see it in people who resent their upbringing and blame their family's situation during their childhood for all their current problems. These people often won't recognize a breakthrough if it slapped them across the face because they are caught in a thought cycle of being a victim of circumstance. Of course, people who have endured a traumatic childhood have every right to address that in adulthood and acknowledge their trauma. However, remaining stuck within it, and playing their trauma and doubt on repeat in their mind only begets more negativity. At a certain point, we grow up and we become fully responsible for what we do, the decisions we make, and how we feel.

You absolutely must take 100% of the responsibility for all of the actions and results in your life and, most importantly, all of the beliefs in your life. You're going to have to make profound shifts in your thinking if you want to reach your goals.

This requires a paradigm shift on your part. A *paradigm* is how we categorize, compartmentalize and define the subject matter we encounter in our lives. Your personal paradigm is the way you choose to define and label what you know and observe. Thus, if your paradigm consists of boxing up all of your responsibilities as the fault of others and the situations around you, that has to change.

Your new paradigm has to shift to one that acknowledges everything you're experiencing as results in your life are because of your choices and beliefs, not anyone else's. You are under no obligation to chain yourself to an old way of thinking. If your paradigms don't serve you, create new ones. You have the power of influence over yourself.

One of the biggest keys to my success has been my ability to influence my mind in a positive way. I knew the power of words through Scripture—both of my parents are pastors. I know that all things are possible for those that believe. When my parents preached that from the pulpit, I believed them. Creating empowering beliefs means that you are not the passenger in your life; rather, you are in the driver's seat. You determine what you put into your life and what comes out. It's not easy at first. When I first began taking action to achieve my success, there were positive books that I was listening to all the time. Eventually, I learned to protect my mind. I stopped watching the news and hanging out with negative people.

LESSON FIFTEEN
PARADIGMS

As I stated before, success has everything to do with the power of words. Whatever you nurture within yourself is what will grow. I chose to believe in the positive words I would hear from the sermons of my parents. I chose to be the captain of my own ship. Self-determinism is directly influenced by your belief in the words you hold fast to. Once I learned the power and influence that positive words had on my overall thought process, it changed the way I spoke to myself and the way I interacted with other people around me. I realized the importance of not letting other people's negativity become my negativity.

Your personal paradigm is the way you choose to define and label what you know and observe.

LESSON SIXTEEN

INFLUENCE YOUR MIND

Success is not a destination; success is a journey. Destination is not just a physical place on a map, it's the state of fulfillment, joy and satisfaction you want to live in. Materialistically speaking, that varies from person to person, so there's no one definition of what a dream destination looks like for all of us. Success is not about hitting the goal, it's about understanding that there is another achievement that you are going to go after. It's continuous and it doesn't stop with the attainment of just one achievement.

The key is understanding the formula versus obtaining the goal. Clarity is power—when something is clear that means that you can actually see it and you can actually hear it.

When you decide what success means to you, don't compare it to anyone else's definition. It's personal. Success to you could be in your relationships, your health, or your finances. It carries over into every part of your life. The clarity of knowing what you want—that's what matters. Here's a target sentence for you to use: "I Am so happy and grateful now that I earn over $12,000 a month."

The Bible says, "He will give you the desires of your heart" (Psalms 37:4).

I spent a lot of time believing I had to go out and get it, but it was within me all along.

How do I make it a burning desire of my heart? The five senses are the way to capture the desires of your heart. You've got to inundate yourself with your success mantra. You've got to inundate your heart with it.

Inundate your senses by placing visuals everywhere. Images around you affect you both subconsciously and consciously. When I surround myself with visuals of my goals and desires, I'm feeding my internal GPS—my reticular activating system—and it's going to go to work for me.

Just as you use your physical GPS to go to a place you haven't gone to yet, use your mental GPS to get to success you don't have in the present yet. See it, feel it, touch it. Visualize seeing your bank's online user platform and instead of seeing the number that is presently available, see $100,000. I used my mental GPS to earn six figures in nine months.

In order to inundate your senses and properly visualize and mentally experience your desired outcomes, your taste has to change to match what life is like for you with what you want. Go to expensive restaurants. Go window shopping for the items you own in your mental image of your desired state of success. My standards of what I wanted would change as I developed my belief and faith. I would go to the dealership and sit in a Bentley. I took pictures of myself sitting in it. I made sure I smelled the leather seats and captured a true memory of that distinct scent. You have to get comfortable with engaging all of your senses in the pursuit of your desire. I always say: "You've got to go there before you can get there."

The Ritz Carlton smells differently than the Motel 6. You wouldn't know that unless you put yourself in the environment of both the Ritz Carlton and the Motel 6. You have to take yourself from wherever you are in this exact present moment, and you have to decide where it is you want to live and what it is you want to experience—then you go there in your mind. It's like daydreaming—except you heighten that daydreaming experience with precise visuals, sensations of touching the things you want, and even smelling the air of the environment of your success. All of this is essentially you making an emotional and physical connection and desire into your heart. If you practice this and implement repetition, the right people, circumstances, and opportunities will show up in your present reality.

After much reflection, I realized that negative emotions originally drove me toward success. But I discovered that I didn't need negative emotions to fuel me. Your ability to take action is predicated on your ability to mentally experience what you want every day. Take an 8 ½ by 11 sheet and write it all out. Put your desires down on paper in block letters. Print out twenty of these statements. Place them in strategic locations around your home.

I don't believe in a vision board. The idea is to progress, to realize what growth looks and feels like—that's what you're looking for. Pick a car that you want—that you believe you should be driving—go to the dealership and sit in that same type of car. It will create a new comfort level for you. Everything around you should reflect what you believe is true for yourself. The soap I bathe with says "Super Rich" on it—I am obsessed with this.

There are two sides of success: the spiritual side and the physical side. Your thoughts, feelings, and emotions make up the spiritual side and the majority—90-99%—of your success is understanding the spiritual side of success.

Only 1-10% of your success comes from the physical side. It's about growing this power in your mind.

A shortcut to building the skill of success is to see what it actually looks like. Go and find those who are the best at what it is you want to do. I found someone who was the best at what I did and I started to model myself after him. Find someone you can model. If you are in real estate, find the best in that industry. Study the characteristics of a leader in your area of interest.

The power of study and repetition cannot be discounted or dismissed in any way. The reason it's so important to practice and repeat feeling and seeing your success is because it starts out as somewhat of an unnatural process. Sure, we've all daydreamed and fantasized before—but this goes beyond that. It's more challenging because it requires your full attention, focus and implementation of your physical senses. It's one thing to daydream about a delicious, cold ice cream on a hot day, visualizing what it looks like. It's another to fully visualize it in every aspect: how it feels to hold the cone in your hand, how you balance it to make sure it doesn't spill as it slowly leaks in the heat, and the sensation of how it feels when the cold, creamy flavor meets your lips. You must practice that same level of visualization with each of your desires.

Make the repetition of studying how to give life and energy to your beliefs and desires over, over, and over again a normal part of your day and then you can begin to teach it to others. Once you begin sharing this knowledge with others, you'll understand why teaching is such a great form of repetition and forces you to examine what you are explaining to someone so that you truly understand it and develop even further in your journey. You must always have the ability to learn and change.

There are two sides of success: the spiritual side and the physical side. Your thoughts, feelings, and emotions make up the spiritual side and the majority—90-99%—of your success is understanding the spiritual side of success.

LESSON SEVENTEEN

THE SUCCESS FORMULA

Everywhere I am, I make sure I am able to see where I'm going. This is the **Self-Confidence Formula**.

Desire + Skill x Faith = Self-Confidence

The aspect of faith within your success formula is so critical. Faith allows you to do the impossible. Faith is truly having confidence. If you understand the success formula, there is absolutely nothing you can't accomplish.

Answer the following questions and plug them into the Self-Confidence Formula:

1. **What is your definite purpose?**
2. **What is the persistent, continuous action you'll take?**

Make this a consistent promise to commit to the action you'll take.

The dominating thoughts in my mind are my desire, an obsession for results, and a focus. You can't go a day without thinking about your goals. Some things cannot be reproduced until they are first produced. You are able to construct your desire through the dominating thoughts in your mind—thus, you give the desires you seek their existence. You are your desires' creator.

PART THREE

Your desire will gradually transform into reality. When you actually attain your goal, there will be another plan and another goal. When a desire becomes clear to you, you can actually see it and actually hear it. Whatever desire I hold in my mind will eventually seek expression through the principle of auto-suggestion.

When you see it, hold onto it in your mind's eye for at least ten minutes daily. You can't do shady deals—your deals have got to be built on truth and justice. By repeatedly holding onto your desire through visualization and expressing gratitude, you naturally attract what you need and the people you need. It will be by means of truth and good faith. You're not taking shortcuts, so you won't end up with a bad deal. Projecting positivity through your repetitive visualization will attract more positivity to you.

When you produce gratitude from your thoughts and actions, when you project appreciation, and when you actually celebrate other people's success, you're attracting more of those things into your life. Faith comes by hearing...but faith works through love. Eliminate hate and jealousy.

If hate and jealousy are emotions you know you have problems with, you need to face that head-on or else you'll never be able to properly visualize and realize your desires. If you experience jealousy or hate, you need to take a personal inventory of why you feel that way. What is the actual source of it? More often than not, the source is not rooted in the person you're feeling negativity towards; it's rooted deep within you. It comes from a primal fear that develops from a sense of lacking. In our modern world, that deep, primal fear often presents itself when we feel that we lack what other people have. In order to not let such negative emotions dominate your repetitive thoughts and poison your belief and faith, you have to confront the source of it within you, then make a concerted effort to repetitively practice projecting the opposite of those negative emotions.

Let's take a material desire for a thought experiment on how to reverse jealousy and hate. Imagine an old acquaintance from your high school makes a social media post about their brand new luxury car—and it happens to be the exact same type of car your best friend desires. Your friend might say things like, "What did he do to get that? I want that car. Why don't I have it? His rich family probably bought it for him. He never has to work for anything. I have to work for everything and I still don't get what I want." Those sentiments are rooted in jealousy and hate. Your friend may not have actually thought, "I hate him for having that car. I deserve that car, not him. Why don't I get things easily like him?" but those statements actually translate to, "I'm jealous I don't have that car. I hate that I don't have that car." Your friend's jealousy and hate are actually all rooted in their own sense of lack. Their sense of insufficiency, envy or dissatisfaction developed from a deeply buried fear—a fear of not having needs met.

Lack, jealousy and hate can emerge from the material or the abstract and intangible. Regardless of the outside source, feeding the negativity of what you're lacking instead of showing gratitude for that person's success will poison your own beliefs and your progress toward success. Remember, you receive the same energy you project. In this hypothetical situation, instead of projecting their deep fear by making those hateful statements, your friend could reverse their negativity by instead saying, "Look at his new car! That's really wonderful. I love that car. I can't wait to get one, too. I hope he enjoys it!"

It's also important to note that this is why spending valuable time on social media can be a slippery slope for your mentality if you're trying to focus on visualizing your desire. Social media has a way of feeding into people's deepest fears of deprivation and insufficiency. It can foster feelings like lack, jealousy, fear and hate. Social media consists of platforms that people often use to show off success. If you're not practicing gratitude and love, you can easily get caught up in experiencing all of that negative energy when looking at other people's posts.

There is insurmountable positive energy to be gained in showing love for others in situations like our hypothetical thought experiment above. There is no reason to have jealousy or hate for other people's abundance because truly, there is an endless source of abundance for every single person. The key is knowing how to believe, how to have faith and how to visualize yourself having already reached your destination. If you are truly focused on your own desires and destination, you won't have time to worry about what others have.

LESSON EIGHTEEN

THE PAIN/ PLEASURE PENDULUM

What do you allow yourself to think about consistently? Are your persistent thoughts rooted in pain or pleasure?

Pain and pleasure are the two drivers of desire. Fundamentally, your motivation for desire can be driven in either a positive or negative way and at its source, that equates to pleasure or pain. Over 80% of all people are driven by overcoming pain.

Only 20% are driven to motivation by pleasure.

Have you stopped to think about what your biggest, deepest fear is? When you write out your deepest fears, you're only touching the surface level of your deepest truths.

Fundamentally, there are only three human fears:

1. Not belonging.
2. Not being loved.
3. Not being good enough.

It is from these three facets of fear that all of our doubt, unhappiness and negativity arises. We wear the cloak of these human fears in a variety of ways—thus, they can take on different aspects and look differently on diverse types of people.

LESSON NINETEEN

YOUR DEEPEST DESIRE AND YOUR BIGGEST FEAR

These fears motivate us, driving us to survive. However, in order to thrive, you have to learn how to address these fears within yourself. You have to learn what these fears look like *on you*. One person may express their fear of not belonging by throwing big parties and constantly socializing while another may become extremely introverted and avoid all social interaction. Even as they exist on opposite ends of the social spectrum, both of their behaviors are rooted in fear.

Fear is a natural part of the human condition as it has helped us survive as a species. However, it becomes a hindrance to achieving our desires when we let it dictate our daily thoughts and behaviors. When fear is at the stern of our ship, we are driven to impatience and faithlessness, and our beliefs fall to the wayside.

Fear becomes a hindrance to achieving our desires when we let it dictate our daily thoughts and behaviors.

LESSON TWENTY
URGENCY MATTERS

"Patience is a virtue" became a saying ingrained in our universal collective not because our ancestors were concerned with others being inconsiderate; rather, it developed to combat fear and what fear creates in our daily lives. Having patience while visualizing and repeating good habits in order to attain a desire is not new or unique to us modern humans. It just looked a lot different over the millennia.

Think for a moment about our ancient, prehistoric ancestors who had to hunt in order to satiate their hunger. They had to employ unquantifiable amounts of patience in order to reap the best reward when hunting. They did not impatiently settle for a small rabbit or yearling. They waited for big game to appear.

They stifled their fear of hunger with patience and it paid off for them and for their communities. They created visual images of what they wanted most in the world. Those images are still present today in the ancient cave paintings from 25,000 years ago, depicting the hunt of stags. Whatever was important to them—whatever they desired—they created visual imagery of it.

Our commitment of waiting for the best kill on a hunt is mirrored by our modernized desire to not settle for just anything simply because it's convenient. Our desire has to be able to ignite that same ancient urgency that exists within us and superimpose it on what we desire presently.

In the end, there is only one core human desire—happiness. What is the purpose of having wants? It is happiness. Therefore, living a life of purpose is the pathway to desire.

Urgency is driven by desire—regardless of whether the desire is rooted in pain or pleasure. Everything you are experiencing today, everything around you and everything you have, are results of the results of forgotten thought efforts. You are experiencing the results of your past thoughts and actions and you may—or may not—realize you put your present reality into place with your thoughts and actions. If you take a moment to think on that, imagine what you could accomplish by applying the tools of belief and faith and making that a daily habit.

It is of the utmost importance to make our desires unstoppable. They need to be crystal clear to all of our senses. Furthermore, you must place a **sense of urgency** around your desire. Without urgency, desire loses all of its value. How driven are you now to drive towards that ideal day? How bad do you *really* want it? This is not something you wait around for and say, "Oh yeah, I'll write down my desires tomorrow."

LESSON TWENTY-ONE

BLESSED ARE THE HUNGRY

The Gospel of Luke teaches us how the hungry get satisfied while the complacent miss out. "Blessed *are you* who hunger now, for you shall be filled. Blessed *are you* who weep now, for you shall laugh" (Luke 6:21). This formula for success has been passed down to you through these ancient teachings. Blessed are those who are hungry because the hungry will do whatever it takes to be satisfied. Hunger, one of our most primal urgencies, is an allegory. It taps into our most primordial needs. It is a blessing because it creates something in us that is so essential to our existence, we have no choice but to address it to survive. Your desires and skills must constantly be increasing. Every day, you should feed your desire. Get hungrier and hungrier until you feel compelled to act.

In our modern world, we have so much at our immediate beck and call. We can order something from the internet and have it delivered the same day. We are able to have food from just about any restaurant near us delivered to our doorstep by tapping on a glass screen. We can think of a song and immediately add it to our playlist and listen to it on repeat—no more buying CDs just to hear one song. No more hoping the radio will play our favorite song while we're in the car.

Our sense of urgency for our desires has been muted by our modern conveniences. In order to combat the dulling of our natural ability to feel urgency, we have to tap into our personal sense of necessity and learn to recognize it, harness it and use it to our advantage. The root of your desire is tied directly to the deep source of your urgency.

Ask yourself again, how badly do you *really* want it? What does it take to activate your elemental sense of urgency? What makes you hungry for it? What drives you to need your desire? Reflect on what urgency really means to you. It is always linked to the root of your desire.

PART FOUR

In our world, the statistics of success for entrepreneurs can look dire if you're only focusing on the numbers. Only 22% of all entrepreneurs actually survive. Of those, only 3% thrive. Keep in mind that there is no reason those statistics must remain the status quo. What could help you become part of the 22%—or even more, what could help you be part of the movement that shifts that percentage to a higher number?

Focus on the following specific skills if you're going to succeed:

1. **Leadership**
2. **Creativity**
3. **Emotional Intelligence**
4. **Communication**
5. **Critical Thinking and Decision-Making**
6. **Persistence**
7. **Deep and Meaningful Interpersonal Relationships**
8. **Cognitive Behavioral Flexibility**
9. **Negotiation and Sales**
10. **Expansion of Your Ability to Become a Visionary**

LESSON TWENTY-TWO

EMBRACE YOUR DEFICIENCIES

Learn to embrace your deficiencies—it is an extremely valuable skill. We all have deficiencies. If you're not sure what your deficiencies might be, take a moment to reflect on aspects of your personality and life where you—or perhaps even others—find fault in yourself. Doing this takes a development of self-awareness, but in the end it will be worth it...even if your feelings get hurt a little. When we are made aware of a personal deficiency, we typically perceive it as a negative trait. This makes it difficult to self-identify and even more troublesome to us if someone else points it out to us. You've got to be able to overcome your ego and acknowledge your deficiencies, otherwise you'll be existing in a state of denial—and there is no growth in denial. When people feel less-than-perfect or less-than-complete, they get sold surface level solutions. You don't need a surface wipe-down to work on your deficiencies; you need a deep clean.

Instead of the surface level solution—acquiring material things like buying a big-screen TV or financing a shiny new vehicle—successful people buy a book. It really is as simple as that. Instead of spending hours of valuable time getting lost watching other people do things on TikTok or Instagram, successful people get lost inside of a library.

Take action toward your shortcomings. Face them head on. Have faith that you noticed them for a reason. Celebrate them, own them, and then you will create power over them.

Make it a daily habit to act as if you cannot fail. Failure is a notion we developed to compensate for our own mismanagement of our time and energy. Failure has a negative connotation because we have intrinsically imprinted our brains with the idea that failure means there is a complete absence of *any* success. That is simply not true. The fact of the matter is failure is not a black-and-white concept. There is a whole gray area within the meaning of failure that yields learning and growth.

What would you do today if you knew there was absolutely no chance you could fail? Dig deep into your mind. Take any scenario and apply this mental activity to it. Here's a personal example: my friend taught his kid how to ride a bike by teaching her how to fall. Most people are taught that falling off a bike equates to failure in riding it. That's simply not true. During the process of learning to ride a bike, you are bound to fall—so it's important to know how to fall the right way: safely. Eventually, you will ride a little further before your next fall, but you will understand what it felt like to glide effortlessly along a road on that bike. You will get back on it, capture that feeling of successfully riding for a distance, and go even further next time. Eventually, you will cycle seamlessly everywhere. You may never fall again! But if you do, you will still know the right way and how to get back up and keep going. This cultivates an attitude that exists in those who are successful—let someone teach you how to fall. Have faith that falling is learning. At no time do I mention that success is about winning. It is about failing and falling forward. Whatever you do, keep getting back on that bike.

To truly believe and maintain your belief, you'll stop making limiting statements like, "It's on its way," or "It's coming."

LESSON TWENTY-FOUR
SMALL CHANGES
=
BIG RESULTS

Small changes over time will ultimately lead to big results. One of the most essential skills of those who are successful is their ability to break big problems down into smaller component parts, making it possible to build wealth. Successful people don't go looking for the one big thing that will make them rich. Rather, they compound small, incremental improvements one percent at a time. It seems small when it's written on paper, but that's the power of compounding. Even if you used the increase of one percent per week, you will exponentially increase in whatever you are doing. Find what a one percent increase for your goal looks like for you. Focus on a one percent increase per day.

Focus on a one percent increase per day.

LESSON TWENTY-FIVE
FAITH REQUIRES PATIENCE

Faith requires patience, and there are no shortcuts for patience. Your desires and your skills are multiplied by your faith. Faith is the seed of patience that you continually plant and nurture. Time is not something God operates on; only humans acknowledge measured time. Faith is having patience that works through love. Envy, anger, impatience—none of these emotions lead to actions that will actually make anything happen faster for you.

A very basic example of how envy, anger and impatience can work against you can be found while waiting in a line at a store. You have your items and you're ready to check out. Everyone in front of you is ready to check out, too. You are no different from any of the other customers. If you become impatient and begin saying negative, angry things about the situation, it won't make the line move faster. If you envy the person who is at the front of the line, it doesn't magically swap you out and put you in their place. Most likely, everyone will just see you as a disgruntled person that they want to avoid. If you check yourself, realize that it is a deficiency on your part to feel this way, and you put your faith into having patience, the entire situation will play out much differently for you. The line may not move any faster, but you will have an improved outlook, others will appreciate you, and, hey, someone might even notice your good energy and let you skip ahead in line!

LESSON TWENTY-SIX

FAITH IN YOUR SUCCESS PLAN

Faith in all realms of your life has to become a solid part of your success plan. Having faith in your success plans doesn't always happen instantly or overnight. That does not mean you should take a break from faith or lose your patience. Patience, love and resilience are key for you to maintain your faith and they allow your return to success—and multiplied success—to come over time. Remember, the life you are experiencing at this very moment while reading this book—both the good and bad aspects—are the fruits of long-past thought patterns and beliefs you have held for quite some time.

You may not have realized what you were creating with your thoughts, but you are living in that creation presently.

Life is a process that we have to go through to *grow* through. Good and bad—although subjective in nature—occur in our life naturally. Nature is balanced in that way. Storms that bring cold fronts with terrible lightning and wind always yield beautiful, crisp cold days.

LESSON TWENTY-SEVEN

SERENITY PRAYER

Ask that you be granted true serenity. Practice the Serenity Prayer, originally written by the American theologian Reinhold Niebuhr. "God, grant me the serenity to accept the things I cannot change, courage to change the things I can, and wisdom to know the difference."

"God, grant me the serenity to accept the things I cannot change, courage to change things I can, and wisdom to know the difference."

Personally, I always add the caveat of, "Grant me the serenity to accept the things that I cannot change—with peace and calm."

Peace and calm—the building blocks of serenity—are key components of faith. I change the things that I can, and I am courageous. I ask to be granted the wisdom to know the difference. Age and wisdom will always trump youth and enthusiasm. Youth often try to change things that are out of their control, but that is a futile struggle.

LESSON TWENTY-EIGHT

YOU ARE THE ANSWER

Part of acknowledging and experiencing serenity is to understand that you are your own answer to problems for which you seek resolve. You are both the problem and solution in your life. You have to develop one hundred percent accountability for your outcomes. The path you are on is one of your own design. Are you going to walk the same path you have been on unconsciously? Or will you forge a new path? Feel and nurture a burning desire in your heart for the path you truly want to walk on. Take small, incremental steps in your success that compound into world-class success. Have you been creating these little wins each day? Enjoy the highs and keep your faith during the lows.

What does keeping your faith *really* mean? We hear that term thrown around a lot, and it seems fairly straightforward, but if you really understood it, you wouldn't be lacking. If you are still looking at your life and saying, "My goals and desires aren't actually real because I can't see any proof of them," then whether you realize it or not, you've convinced yourself there's only a *possibility* that they will come to pass, but you actually have real faith that your desires will become your reality. If you were actually keeping your faith, you wouldn't continue to search for proof. If you've got your phone in your hand, then you're not wandering around looking for it—you know it's there because you feel it and can see it. That works the same for anything else you could feel or see.

Part of practicing keeping the faith is remembering that you don't actually search for proof of things you believe in. For example, you know the sun rises in the east every morning. That is not something you doubt. You don't go check to make sure it actually came to pass every morning or search for evidence of it. Whether or not it will come to pass doesn't ever worry you. You're sure of it, you're confident in it, you KNOW it. You aren't guessing or worrying about it. That's where you must be with your desire. This type of faith is what it means to believe, and what it means to keep the faith.

There will be moments where you'll feel you really need to see some sign of a result in order to give yourself some proof of your desire.

That is only an indication that you truly don't believe in what you're telling yourself. You truly don't believe you are creating your life. You don't know that consciousness is the only reality. You are still looking for something outside of yourself for answers! No good.

You manifest what you are, not what you want. I don't wake up every morning and affirm "I live in New Jersey. I live in New Jersey. I live in New Jersey." I KNOW it so therefore, it is. To get rid of the looking for proof or having anxiety, remind yourself you are creating your life every moment of the day. Your life will only show you what you believe to be true. When you say something like, "I know my affirmations are true," that's great. You know it, therefore your life will show it. BUT the minute you finish off your story with, "It's not actually true. I'm not getting results," your life will respond, "Okay, they're saying it's not true so I have to show them that they are right."

LESSON TWENTY-NINE

THE WHEEL OF LIFE

What we do in one area of our life echoes through all areas of our life. Take the creation of your powerful vision as an example. If purpose is the reason *why* we do things, our vision is the tangibility that shows us *how* to do it.

We need to be able to develop a solid vision in all areas of our life because each part of our life has an effect on the other. Each spoke in our wheel of life represents a unique aspect. If one of those spokes were to break, the integrity of the entire wheel is compromised. Life goes on, the wheel keeps turning, pressures come and go. There are inevitable peaks and valleys and it's important to not forget that.

Every area in our lives is constantly in a state of flow.

Life is also a wheel of fortune. Some people are luckier than others—but luck isn't promised, and it's also not guaranteed to last. Relying on luck alone isn't a part of faith. Successful people spin their life's wheel of fortune again and again until they get the success that they want. People who we consider having been born lucky may not realize they can spin their wheel of fortune. They may stay stagnant—or even worse, if a spoke breaks, they may not realize they have the power and belief to fix it.

The spokes of your wheel can be summarized as the following areas of your life:

1. **Romantic Relationships**
2. **Other Relationships**
3. **Fun and Recreation**
4. **Physical Environment/Place**
5. **Personal Growth**
6. **Business/Career**
7. **Financial Situation**
8. **Health**

Take a moment to rate yourself in each of these areas. Using a scale of one through ten (ten being the highest, one being the lowest), assess what number you believe you are currently at. Keep that information on hand, as it will help you understand which spoke on your wheel might be in need of repair.

LESSON THIRTY

TRAFFIC LIGHT SYSTEM

Think of your success in these areas like a traffic light system. Success is doing ordinary things extraordinarily well. Once you've rated yourself in all of the areas, apply the traffic light system to them—red, yellow, and green.

If an area of your life is lacking, color it with red. Color the areas in your life where you are just doing alright with yellow. For the areas in life where you are doing well, color those green. Determine the yellow areas that you need to keep an eye on while correcting the red and maintaining the green.

Using the traffic light system helps bring a universal visual to these important spokes on your wheel of life, and it will help you identify what is most urgent to attend to and what you're doing well.

Only 3% of the population actually write down all of their goals.

Yet with all of the successful people in the world, 95% have written their goals down. Coincidence? I think not. Statistics around successful goal setting have been around since at least the 1950s. Eight percent of those who wrote their goals down hit their set target. Within that 8%, seven things they specifically did differently from others to guarantee their success were identified:

1. They start with the end in mind.
2. They build a support system around themselves.
3. They set goals that are specific and also challenging.
4. They recognize when they are procrastinating.
5. They use interval training — 20 minutes on —maximum performance.
6. They listen to music.
7. They understand that multitasking is a myth.

LESSON THIRTY-ONE

TANGIBILITY

Creating your vision is just as important as the words you hear and speak. Vision is an actual, real thing and it becomes tangible. Maintaining and meditating on your vision keeps you focused at all times. By envisioning, you are able to turn the intangible into the tangible. We must create something that is not only highly desirable to us, but is so clear that we think in our minds that we can reach out and touch it. Consider all your goals and ideas in the wheelbarrow thought tactic—are they tangible enough that I could actually put them in the wheelbarrow?

There is a simple method to practice creating an effective vision if you're a beginner. Close your eyes and imagine a lemon. You can see it—it's perfectly clear to you. It's yellow and perfectly ripe. It sits right in front of you. You reach out and pick up the lemon with your right hand. You know what it feels like, so you're able to imagine feeling it in your hand—its texture, its weight. You squeeze it and notice that you can feel it give ever so slightly. You raise it up to your nose and sniff it. There's a light citrus scent. Now, you do something you normally don't do, and you bite into that lemon. You hear your teeth sink into it and you feel your mouth pucker. It's sour! You feel your tastebuds react to the bitter acidity. Your mouth waters.

You just had a physical reaction to a mental vision.

That is the power of having a vision. If you can make yourself physically react to an imagined lemon, you can do it with absolutely anything else in the physical world—you just have to believe.

Charge your vision with the power of your physical senses so that it develops into a life of its own.

LESSON THIRTY-TWO
WRITE IT DOWN

The pen is mightier than the sword; it is mightier than the keyboard. There is a lot of power in handwritten notes. Putting a pen in your hand and having a physical connection to the paper creates a psychological connection. In turn, that creates a powerful emotional connection as we make it through our adult years. It creates real emotive experiences.

(Habakkuk 2:2)

LESSON THIRTY-THREE

REPETITION REPETITION REPETITION

Beyond implementing this level of vision, understand that repetition is the mother of all skills. You must learn to repeat your vision so clearly and palpably that you can reach out and touch it. You have to practice reaching out and touching your vision every single day. You need to read what you wrote in your journal every single day. You need to look at the pictures of your goals at least once a day, every day. Successful execution of this one skill—repetition—is so simple but it is often completely ignored.

Repetition isn't a new concept. It has been around throughout recorded civilization. Take rosary beads, for example. Those who pray using rosary beads repeat prayers with the same beads until they are cemented in their heart. Japamala beads date back at least to the 3rd or 4th century in China and are used as repetition prayer beads as well. Their origin is thought to be so ancient that no certain date can be placed on their use. Repetition has been a known tool for creating desired realities since recorded history.

"Ask and you shall receive" (Matthew 7: 7,8), tells you that you shall receive. You have to think about time as it is described in verse eight. Time as we think about it doesn't actually exist. What actually exists is whatever you're perceiving in the present moment—right *now*. The past has already passed and the future hasn't happened yet. So how do you measure time in terms of when your reality matches your affirmations and your visualizations? The same way you measure time regardless—with language. You apply meaning to a word, and that meaning becomes one with the combination of letters in a word and the sounds you make to pronounce it.

Our word for measurement for the time it takes for your belief to become your reality is the word *and*. *And* is the period of time it will take to make your desired future come to pass. "Ask and you shall receive," actually makes this apparent with the placement of "and" in the sentence. What do you do during *and*? You celebrate that you're getting what you asked for! Celebrate it as if you already have it—because it is already yours from the moment you truly believed and asked for it.

If you accomplish something of importance to you, like getting a new car when you've previously had to take the bus...you don't think about taking the bus anymore and you don't say, "I wish I had a car." You already have it. It is done. That is the same application you should use for whatever it is you desire for your successful future. Do not allow yourself to feel any worry or lack about the three-dimensional world around you and whether or not your present reality shows hints or signs of your desire becoming your reality. If you've got faith and belief and you are taking the actions necessary—which include celebrating what is coming to you because it's yours—it's impossible to continue to worry about it.

LESSON THIRTY-FOUR
SURVIVE TO THRIVE

It is important to not only set your desires, but also to know when to set your desires on *guide* mode. Each of us has our own inner visualization of our needs and we rank them from least important to most important without even realizing it. One way you can self-assess what your most important needs are is to look at what you focus on the most for your own self-sustenance. Is food something you think of constantly? Do you worry about where you live more than anything else? Does a lack of respect in your current career bring a recurring negative thought pattern into your life that you know you need to learn to shake off? If your personal hierarchy of needs is out of order, then your *I Am* is difficult for you to believe in with full faith.

In 1943, psychologist Abraham Maslow created the Hierarchy of Needs. It demonstrates the stages that we all go through in our lives. First, we need to survive in order to thrive. We seek air, water, food, shelter, sleep, clothing and reproduction. These are fundamental to the human condition—the most primitive needs we all have as humans. Thriving must occur psychologically as well. Pain turns into thriving. Sometimes, it's okay to be in survival mode. It's natural. That pain drives us. In fact, it is often necessary. But in order to bring yourself the success you want, you must psychologically shift from surviving to thriving. You don't want to spend your entire life at the bottom of Maslow's pyramid, stuck in survival. Make the decision to thrive now.

After those basic needs, Maslow lists safety needs (personal security, employment, resources, health and property) as the next step in the order of hierarchy. These safety needs are essential to survival. But ask yourself how you can address your safety needs from a mode of thriving as opposed to surviving. Do you want to stay in a dead-end, life-draining job simply because you need to survive? Of course, have gratitude for employment—but don't settle in your own unhappiness. You are allowed to create a vision for your idea of ideal safety needs.

Love and belonging are third on Maslow's hierarchical scale, and, undoubtedly, we as humans thrive off of feeling loved and feeling like we belong. Maslow lists friendship, intimacy, family and a sense of connection as the defining attributes of this level. But what if you apply his given characteristics to yourself—gratitude for yourself—as well as gratitude for the friendships and connections you already have in order to visualize and create even more love and belonging? Do not feel that you must limit yourself. You are able to visualize and make tangible your most ideal love and sense of belonging.

Esteem is second to the top of the pyramid according to Maslow. It is comprised of respect, self-esteem, status, recognition, strength and freedom. All of these are actually part of what encompasses your goals, the creation of your goals, your belief and your faith. People will study Maslow's hierarchy of needs and not actually understand that they have a say-so about how esteem looks in their life. Instead of wishes and longing for the attributes of esteem to exist, they can be made into your reality by your energy alone. Many people study Maslow and believe their esteem has to come from outside sources—but it is the exact opposite. All of the attributes of esteem come to you from your I Am.

Lastly, Maslow tops his hierarchy with self-actualization. Self-actualization means transcendence. What you want to do by creating your vision for your success is transcend your current reality and shift into your desired state of reality with what you've envisioned for yourself becoming tangible. He defines self-actualization as the desire to become the most that one can be. What does that mean to you? What does that mean to a person presented with this hierarchy in a psychology class? Is it just viewed as theory to most people? The thing about theory is you must put it into practice. If everyone adhered to Maslow's hierarchy and understood that the absolute most important need was to become the best, most successful version of oneself, then perhaps there wouldn't be so many people still stuck at the bottom of his pyramid, in constant survival mode, sometimes shifting into safety needs.

Essentially, what Maslow has given us is a pyramid of visualization that demonstrates that our belief and faith in our own success and desires is our most important need. It is a matter of putting it into practice. Use your mind's eye to create your vision of your I Am, implement repetition, and you will master your own self-actualization. It won't merely be a need for you—it will be who you are.

LESSON THIRTY-FIVE
YOUR SENSES

Your memories establish the past, your senses perceive the present, and your imagination shapes the future. Senses in the present moment drive us towards our goals and aspirations. It can be as simple as smelling food cooking in the present moment and feeling your stomach rumble, which in turn motivates you to take action and eat food. Goals bring your imagined visions from the future and draw them deep down into the present moment so that it is real for you right now—all through the physical sense.

There are up to twenty-one different senses in the human body, and arguably more than that from scientific standpoints. Some of these senses are so common, we don't even realize they're part of what makes up our senses. For example, we perceive pain through nociception, we balance ourselves through our equilibrioception sense and we have an overall sense of body awareness when we close our eyes and touch our nose—which is called proprioception.

When you can identify what your dominant sense is, it becomes exponentially more real and powerful to you in the present moment. When you are visualizing, you want to make sure that you are incorporating all five of your physical senses: taste, smell, touch, sound and sight. Recall the lemon exercise from Lesson Sixteen. To successfully practice that visualization exercise, you had to implement all five of your physical senses. If you practiced the exercise correctly, there was never a physical lemon in front of you, but it didn't matter to your senses. They didn't know the difference between your actual and perceived sensations.

When you develop your vision of the exact life you want to live, you've got to give *sense* to all aspects of it in all of its colors. In doing this, it's extremely important to make sure that the last thing you visualize is your *dominant sense*. Within your visualization of your desire, focus on what the dominant sense of that desire is. It will vary depending on your specific desire. This is an example of an action you must take to realize your visualization into your material world. Remember, we can be action takers or excuse makers, but we can never be both.

LESSON THIRTY-SIX

ENERGIZED DESIRES

Energizing your desire is just as important as identifying the dominant sense. Fuel your desires and charge them up with energy. Charge your vision with the power of your physical senses so that it develops into a life of its own.

The most important word of a question is not the first word, but the second word, that is usually a verb (action word) and not a pronoun (I, you, he, she we, they). *Can, could, should, must, will* typically begin a question. But pay close attention to the second word that you are using. Put this theory into practice.

Take this question: Can I make a $100,000 annual salary? Break that question down. Scratch through the first word. It should look like, "~~Can~~ I make a $100,000 annual salary?" You're left with, "I make a $100,000 annual salary?" Remove the interrogative punctuation. Now you've got, "I make a $100,000 annual salary."

There is so much more power in the second part of that sentence. The importance is in the action, the verb. Amplify your questions by repeatedly taking out the interrogative word and making it into a statement. In turn, the amplification of your words will empower your senses.

LESSON THIRTY-SEVEN

PEAK PERFORMANCE STATE

Our personal peak performance states are created by our psychology and are tied into our senses. This state is demonstrated by what actions you take when things aren't working out for you. When something goes bad, does it define you or destroy you?

You can use what seems like a negative situation as a tool to strengthen you. Like all transformative skills, it takes repetition. You have to identify what you do when you are not feeling positive. You can understand that your faith is having a moment and is wavering, but you don't have to let your wobbly faith thrive. You can get it back in fighting form. One of the first steps in doing so is simply recognizing it and being aware that your faith needs a boost. It isn't detrimental to simply recognize it—you don't have to view your recognition of it as a negative thought. Instead, upon recognizing an issue with your faith, have gratitude for your ability to be able to notice there is an issue. Then you can move forward and address it correctly without dwelling and reinforcing negativity, which creates entire negative thought patterns.

Without the mental tools to address it, when our faith goes south, our whole formula implodes. Change happens in an instant—successful people know how to make this happen. What we are feeling and how we are acting are connected to one another. If you act like your inner faith and belief has imploded, that will inevitably become apparent as a change of your whole self on the outside.

Stand tall, be proud, keep smiling, and stay invigorated. Our physiology determines our psychology. Regardless of what bump in the road you encounter, maintain your physical state of one who exudes success and power. Exuding the best, most powerful version of yourself physically will, in turn, fuel your emotional state which affects your senses.

PART FIVE

LESSON THIRTY-EIGHT

WHAT IS PROFIT?

Believe Nation was born at a very challenging time for the world. March 28, 2020—at the epicenter of the pandemic—perfect time to pivot for profits. The birth of Believe Nation has brought profit to people's lives. So many people think that profit is just about money. Take a product or service and add value to it—such as Leadership or Mindset, and relationships will profit from it.

Take a product or service and add value to it — such as Leadership or Mindset, and relationships will profit from it.

LESSON THIRTY-NINE
THE PIVOT

Believe Nation was born in the midst of challenge. So we had to **pivot**—learn to shift and change the way we do business. A *pivot* is defined as making a turn. We are making a turn and shift in how you are going to see things.

Pivot in how you think about the pandemic. Shift to thinking about it in a different way—there are people who have thrived and succeeded irrespective of the challenges the pandemic brought. There were people who were able to make a pivot. The goal is not just about your bank account; rather, it involves every area of your life.

pi•vot: **to shift and change the way business is done; making a turn that will affect the way you see things**

LESSON FORTY
IT STARTS WITH ME

I believe that we are always just beginning. Stay in that mode of learning and beginner's zone. Open yourself up to learning and growing—even after you become successful. This is not a destination; it's a journey of growth to become all that God has intended for you to become.

The best teachers are always eternal students. Humbly sit before a teacher. Practice the Pillars of Pivot to Profit:

1. **Leadership**
2. **Financial Wellness**
3. **Health and Fitness**
4. **Spirituality**
5. **Mindfulness and Emotional Strength**
6. **Family, Friends and Relationships**
7. **Purpose and Personal Growth**

I believe that these are all equally important. Whenever there is a breakdown in a person's life—it is typically tied to one or more of these areas. If you don't know what these areas are it will be difficult to pinpoint the issue and integrate a formula for pivoting.

LESSON FORTY-ONE

IT'S ALL CONNECTED

There is always a root cause. My life changed when I realized that my physical world was dictated by my spiritual, inner world. There is a pivotal moment when there is an issue in one's life. There are pillars that are all connected to hold up that person—those pillars can be found as support systems for your unlimited belief.

There always needs to be someone that I'm listening to to learn more and grow. Put the blueprint in place by identifying your blind spots—your limited beliefs.

Quit trying to solve the problem yourself with outside eyes.

Use your spiritual eyes. They are what allow you to have your mind's eye.

LESSON FORTY-TWO

THE FOUNDATION IS FAITH

This is where it all starts—the connection to a Higher Power. If you live only on the physical plane of life, that is going to be a very difficult life. If I did, my life would be controlled by other people, the events of this world, what other people had to say. However, I am the one that dictates how my world is actually created. My words have the ability to change what I see in the physical world. Being able to respond versus reacting—words create everything.

Faith in all realms of your life has to become a solid part of your success plan.

LESSON FORTY-THREE

CRISIS OF FAITH

FEAR—having a fear attack. The way we are going to address it and take Pivot to Profit is by taking inventory on who and what you've been listening to. Faith and fear are driving determinants of your success or your lack of success. I want you to believe in something that's not part of your present reality, something that has not actually happened yet. The amount of time you put into fear can actually create it. It's all in your heart—if you take away the letter F in fear, you have the word (h)ear. Whenever you speak that fear, you will create more of it. Irrespective of what is happening in the physical world, you have to control your inner world. When I finally learned this, I was literally in tears for nine days. You may not be able to see the changes immediately, but they will occur.

I posit that fear is what stops people from creating their desired reality for themselves—fear of success—not even fear of failure. Well, what if it works? A lot of people are afraid of that. One of the points of sharing my knowledge of this power with you is so you understand that you can only go where you can see. It's as if you've been driving in the fog. You know where you want to go. You've probably already been there. You've seen other people get there but it's impossible for you to physically see.

LESSON FORTY-FOUR

SUCCESS STORIES

You don't have to only take my word for the wonders that applying these techniques in this book work. There are many other people who have taken this information and applied it in their lives in order to experience all of their desires. Remember, there is unlimited abundance available to tap into. Don't fail yourself by believing that there are finite amounts of success and that it's divided up amongst certain people. Your power of I Am is everyone's power, and there is no shortage of I Am.

DON BENJAMIN

Don Benjamin was born in Chicago, but later moved to Minnesota in his childhood. His mom, who was raising Don by herself, wanted to get him away from the harsh realities of the South Side of Chicago.

Growing up, Benjamin always had a tremendous love for basketball. He had always had the feeling that there was something much bigger for him in life than what his general surroundings may have otherwise indicated. Piggybacking off of this itch that there was much more to come for him, he decided to move to Los Angeles and take up his interest in the entertainment industry.

He took a loan out for college and quit his job at a furniture store. Determined to accomplish his dreams, he decided to pursue his passion—an acting, modeling, and music career. It was because of the struggles he had experienced in his life that he was driven to take a different path than what others had expected of him and to completely lock into his focus and become great at something.

Originally, his desire was a career in basketball, but that didn't work out. Benjamin didn't receive the college basketball offers that he hoped for. It was upon this perceived failure that he switched gears and shifted his mentality, putting his energy and attention into success in the complex world of entertainment.

Benjamin never thought, "This isn't going to work out." He had no Plan B or C. He had tunnel vision. He devoted his energy, belief and actions to his desire.

It took Benjamin about seven years to get a big break. Throughout that time, he maintained patience and took an office job in Orange County. He realized that taking no action in the interim wouldn't serve him. He did clerical work like removing staples out of packets and filing papers. In the meantime, Benjamin would visit various modeling and entertainment agencies, trying to lock down representations. Headshots are necessary in the acting and modeling world, but photography can be quite expensive, so Benjamin worked out ways to get photoshoots without any out-of-pocket cost to him. He took roles as an extra in many movies, sometimes for amounts as little as thirty or forty dollars a day in order to make ends meet—all the while not relinquishing his end goal or becoming discouraged.

Benjamin had a true, burning desire inside of him.

"Every time I would start to see myself breaking down and getting discouraged, it's like there was a little voice inside of me that would pick me back up."

He continually recognized that working in entertainment was his calling and that he needed to stick it out and see it through. He didn't dwell on his moments of disappointment or discouragement. Consistently and persistently, he envisioned living in his desired future. Sometimes, Benjamin would call home to his mother for inspiration and encouragement. Having that encouragement from his mom was a way to reinforce his desire. The voice in his head would always tell him that he had no other option—nothing past Plan A—because the last thing he wanted to do was to move back to Minnesota. By denying himself other, more easily attainable goals, he created an urgency for his desire.

Over time, Benjamin noticed that he got little signs from God along the way. He knew he was on the right journey and needed to persist and not even consider giving up.

He spent a great deal of his extra time researching many successful people in the industry and he studied how long it took them to reach their goals. He learned that for most of them, it took ten, twelve, even fifteen years before they really got their break.

That newfound knowledge underscored the importance of emotional strength as a pillar of success. It gave him more assurance that he had the stamina, patience and mental fortitude it took to endure the present time he was in while envisioning his success. He realized that none of the time in between when he began until that moment was wasted—it was actually an opportunity to have more time to continue taking action toward his goal.

People like Don Benjamin, who have the emotional strength to handle setbacks and disappointments, ultimately come out successful. Benjamin's words, imagery and his environment allowed him to stay on the path. It is so important to put yourself in the right environment in order to see success. In Benjamin's case, that meant taking the action of moving to Los Angeles—the absolute, undisputed home of the entertainment industry—while working toward his end goal. His action was extremely paramount to his success. Just like an aspiring marine biologist wouldn't choose to pursue their goal while living in Kansas, Benjamin knew that moving to Los Angeles was an essential step for him, even before he had booked a gig.

From Don Benjamin's experience, we learn that we have got to take inventory of ourselves in order to ensure that we have the right people in our life. Otherwise we run the risk of expending our energy on people that will attempt to take us down.

He utilized social media in a positive way to build his business and brand. He had a PalmPilot when a friend first told him about people that were getting free clothes just for posting themselves wearing the clothes on Instagram. He couldn't even access Instagram on his PalmPilot!

But he pursued this new, attainable goal. He was told he needed to grow a following on social media, then he could reach out to brands and, based on the size of his platform, they would give him free clothes to post about. That had an immediate appeal to him. It was a bite-sized chunk of success that he could strive for and attain while working towards his ultimate goal.

Don upgraded to an iPhone and created an Instagram account. At first, he was uncomfortable with taking selfies. It was an adjustment to learn how to take the best ones and what to write in the captions to gain traction, but eventually, he successfully posted his selfies on Instagram and his page went viral. In a short amount of time, his following quickly grew to over 10,000 followers.

For Benjamin, utilizing social media was key. It was imperative that he learn to use certain hashtags and write certain types of comments to push his posts to appear on the popular "For You" page. He learned that replying to followers and comments on his posts created more engagement on each of his posts and that, in turn, accelerated the growth of his following.

Benjamin received his first big break on *America's Next Top Model* in 2013.

He was leaps and bounds ahead of his competition in terms of popularity before he even filmed the first episode. "I had fifty thousand followers at that time, other contestants had like five hundred followers. The hustler mentality took over in terms of my drive for engagement on Instagram," he explained.

Benjamin signed with the prominent modeling company Wilhelmina. His following on social media grew to over two million.

Today, a lot of people who are gaining followers on social media are either in comedy or they work in motivation because presently, we are in dark times with the pandemic and the troublesome issues in the world. Social media has become the new commercial space. Given the stigma that has developed about the negativity associated with the use of social media, users and consumers have become more conscious about ensuring they produce and consume positive content over time.

Over the past few years, Benjamin has committed himself to reading and growing even more. Growth and development are key factors in not only maintaining your desired success but developing it even further than you originally envisioned. He watched YouTube videos and listened to Bob Proctor and Les Brown.

Benjamin had always been aware of these practices, but after he devoted time and energy to his growth and understanding of these lessons, he is now one hundred percent fully committed to his own self-development and personal growth.

When someone is seeking to grow and better themselves, Benjamin believes that it is all about marketing; it's all about eyeballs. How many people can you get to look at your content? Currently, it's the cheapest way to market oneself successfully.

Benjamin also discussed the importance of

consistency when doing anything. If it's a passion—if it's something you are passionate about and great at—he believes you will do well at it.

His overall purpose is to be as creative as he possibly can be and to help as many people learn that they can be creative, too. He realized that so many people get discouraged—as opposed to encouraged—by what they see on social media. That is why it is important to always move in love, creativity, and positivity.

Benjamin has written a book titled *My Truth*, available on Amazon, where he chronicles his journey to success and becoming a faithful, God-fearing man through raw truth and candid experience.

IVAN TAPIA

Ivan Tapia was born and raised in Tijuana, Mexico. His father was a pharmacist and his mother made a career as a nurse. Ever since he could remember, he had dreamed of becoming a baseball player.

Tapia graduated from high school in the United States. He went on to study at San Diego State University, focusing on engineering. He graduated with a degree in Civil Engineering. On December 12 of 2009, he lost his job. He had recently purchased a home, but upon the job loss, he didn't have the funds to pay his mortgage or even his car note. This was a harsh blow to Tapia's ego—for his entire able-bodied life, he had always worked.

To make ends meet, he began working at a hotel in the San Diego area at La Jolla beach and tennis club. He became accustomed to receiving tips anywhere in the amount of fifty to one hundred dollars at a time—just for carrying around the luggage of wealthy patrons. Through his job, he began to experience wealth with his physical senses. He took those mental experiences and formed visual images, creating a sensory visual representation of the successful lifestyle he wanted.

Tapia believes that his innate desire to be great emerged from what he experienced due to his mind having already had the sensory experience of the wealth and success he wanted.

Through believing in his vision and having faith in it, Tapia cleared out any existing negative paradigms he harbored around rich people—like the notion that wealthy people were often difficult and arrogant. He discovered that wealthy people were nice people. He took action to ensure he could be around those people at every given opportunity. By changing his paradigm, he became more open to the multitude of opportunities available to him to immerse himself in his dream environment around the right people.

Tapia's first experience of serious pain came in his financial life when he lost his civil engineering job. From that, his persistent thoughts and motivations were rooted in pain, not pleasure.

Even as a civil engineer, Tapia realized there was a lid on his potential. But he thought of the Mexican idiom, "The cow that gave me the milk got killed," and he understood that he had been trapped before he lost his job.

He made a routine trip to the bank after having been let go and the sensation of guilt for not being a provider anymore washed over him. During the subsequent weeks and months, Tapia would get up anywhere between 6:00 – 8:00 a.m. each morning in order to sell things on the streets of Mexico so he could financially survive. Through taking this action, he discovered that pain can turn into inspiration. Pain moves you into action mode. He understood it was a root cause of motivation for him. More profoundly, he also realized he did not want to go back to that feeling of pain. For him, suffering and pain had become a signal that something great was going to happen in his life.

"I discovered that I needed to take massive action. I

needed to do things differently." A friend invited me into entrepreneurship through means of network marketing. "I went all in," he explained. The rest is nothing but success!

GARY MCSWEEN

The Power of Believing, even through tough times of hardship, is the key takeaway from the following testimony of Gary McSween.

"From 2014 to 2016, I faced tough times and hardship. God has revealed to me why I went through what I went through. You feel like you're the only person that's going through it. I believed that God could turn around my circumstances. I was reminded of who my Source is," Gary McSween stated.

McSween explained that he can't stress the importance of writing goals down. "My wife and I—we declare our goals aloud together. I started to create a lot more of what I wanted as opposed to what I was seeing."

He reiterated that in order to achieve your desired success, you want to be around others who are encouraging. "I am glad that I went through what I went through because I can speak to anyone. I understand

and have a better perspective of what others are going through. You can turn around your situation if you believe. Words can turn your situation around."

McSween firmly believes we have all been placed on earth for a purpose. We didn't just show up. There is a greater power living inside of each of us.

McSween says that his wife is his "Silver Bullet" force. "She never complained and was always optimistic during the tough times we went through." She is an avid believer in the word of God, in the power of blessing and of being a prayer warrior. "She's a blessing and I wouldn't be where I am without her."

Based on his experience, he explains that one of the greatest days of a person's life is when they decide on the life they truly want for themselves and begin to create it. He drives home the importance of making your goal, writing it down, finding or taking pictures of what it is that you want, and building it in your mind and on paper.

He stressed the power of true, unwavering belief and that whatever you believe, that is what will come to pass. It all lies within creation mode. In order to create, one must start watering the seeds with specific words and actions. "You can create the life that you want," he emphasized.

McSween also pointed out that you can get really creative when you are broke. It creates the necessary, primally instinctive sense of urgency to survive and, in turn, it fosters a willingness to do whatever it takes to win, to pay the full price.

DARRYL DRAKE

In discussing his road to success, Darryl Drake stresses the power of your environment, including the words, images, and people within your environment, and stresses how they impact your present life.

Drake explained that feeling good is a strategy and it must be intentional in terms of your decisions, otherwise other negative thoughts can creep into your mind and begin a pattern of looping.

He credits Stormy Wellington for having a prominent impact on his life and who he's become in the process. Through her guidance and his application of her teachings, he learned how to grow, think and exist in the world of entrepreneurship. When asked to describe the impact her teachings had, Drake said, "She has been that bridge from where I was to where I wanted to be."

"You've got to be willing to do an inventory of who

you're surrounding yourself with," he stated, lending further credence to the importance of doing an in-depth and sometimes uncomfortable inventory of your limiting beliefs.

Furthermore, he stresses the importance of information for personal growth and building your belief system. "The first book I picked up was *How to Win Friends and Influence People* by Napoleon Hill."

Next, he watched the video version of *The Secret*. "It taught me how to think and that 80% of success is what is happening inside of you."

The third book that profoundly impacted him was *The Slight Edge* by Jeff Olsen. Drake claims that book "touches upon doing the right things consistently so that it compounds."

Experiences are also an extremely important key to Drake's notable success. "What are you experiencing on a regular basis? It is about the things that you do in order to see where you want to be even before you can afford it."

Drake also emphatically credits the importance of visualizing and going to places that make you feel good physically. For him, spending time on Malibu Beach or

Newport Beach helped his visualization. He was able to find out where the open houses were in order to tour them and gain a real, physical experience of them. He made it a point to walk in as though it was his own house.

Trips to the Bentley dealership became a regular habit of his. Although he drove a 2007 Chevy Impala, he explains that in his mind, it was his Bentley. "The universe will give you exactly what you work for, are in alignment with, and what you desire."

Drake doesn't leave out the importance of work ethic when recounting the journey to his present success. You absolutely have to do what Darryl Drake did. "You gotta do the work at the end of the day. How to build your business: strengthen relationships in your space. Always doing something that takes me toward my desire."

TWILER PORTIS

Twiler's experience is an important example of the power we have in overcoming setbacks.

Born and raised in Washington, Louisiana—a town too small for a traffic light—Twiler was the child of a teenage mother. Eventually, her parents made the decision to relocate to Houston for a chance at a better life in a bigger city. Twiler stayed behind with her grandmother in Louisiana until fourth grade before moving to Houston to her parents. That time being raised by her grandmother helped develop a distinct character within Twiler.

"My dad was an entrepreneur—he started a construction company. Mom worked at the hospital as a cashier. My dad was very involved in my life—he attended all my track events. I learned from him that I wanted to own my own time and be my own boss."

At eighteen years old, Twiler took up work at a hospital—the corporate American healthcare system—and worked in that world for ten years. She eventually met a great guy that introduced her to network marketing. After she delved into it, she never went back to college.

During her experience with her first company, she learned how to close sales. That experience helped her to develop into the person she is today.

Through network marketing, "I was introduced to goal setting and dream building through multiple MLM experiences, although it wasn't initially making any money," she recounted.

That experience underscored the importance of treating people the way she wanted to be treated. It helped demonstrate to her the level of respect and kindness that was necessary in order to foster success.

Twiler expounds the importance of work ethic when describing her success. "It's very important. It comes with sacrifice—now—but not forever. Roll up your sleeves and do the work because there are no shortcuts. Work smart because there are no shortcuts. Find your champions and mentors."

It was through the loss of her husband that she truly learned how to overcome setbacks. "I was equipped with a strong mindset, constitution, and my Heavenly Father. That's what got me through. My mind was solid—I was prepared. You have to control your mind and thoughts. Otherwise you will fall into a depression."

No matter what the obstacles may be, Twiler encourages everyone to develop a mantra. "To be absent from the body is to be present with the Lord." At one point, she realized she had to slow down in order to actually feel *into* her life.

She notes that adversity will always reveal who is truly in your circle. "Relationship building is key because a successful business is about people. I learned early in my field that I didn't just want 'commission friends.'"

"I always felt like I had to do a little bit more in life in order to achieve success," she continued, highlighting the importance of taking action.

Her experience in overcoming adversity touches on the importance of avoiding negative feelings like lack and jealousy. In her musings on her road to overcoming adversity and becoming her vision of success, Twiler underlined the veracity of the old saying, "Comparison is the thief of joy."

"Looking forward to 2021, my focus is to run my own race and be true to who I am. I don't veer off. It's important to have a clear-cut vision of where you are going amid all of the distractions of the times. Never compare your weaknesses to someone else's strengths."

These accounts of success given by such outstanding people are a testament to the perseverance it takes to be successful during difficult times. Each one of them had a unique, but relatable, trial to overcome.

A common occurrence amongst people who are just getting started in network marketing is hitting a wall of negativity and doubt when discussing their dreams and goals with friends and family. Many times, their friends and family are the first people that are going to tell them that what they're trying to do won't work. They'll ask, "Why are you doing that?" or say, "You're wasting your money," or "You're going on another one of those trainings?"

I believe that before you get there you must go there. And whatever it is that you experience in your life, you believe. So because you experience walking in that home, because you experience driving over there, even though it may seem as though it wasn't real, your belief system, and your body, don't know what's real and what's not. You may ask, "David, can you explain that?" Well, if you've ever had a dream where somebody was chasing you, and you woke up right before they caught you, you realize your body was sweating. Your heart was beating really, really fast. You were still in the comfort of your own bedroom, but your body had no way of knowing if it was real or not. So you experienced that dream. I would go to the Bentley dealership all the time, sit in the car, smell the leather and handle the steering wheel.

Someone might have a mom that's completely

disempowering. Should they not talk to their family? Should they completely disavow their family? I believe that there should be a season of separation. It's not the same as disowning and going no-contact with friends or family, but there has to be a **season of separation.**

When I was beginning my journey and I was living with my dad, I would come home after prospecting all day or doing presentations all day and instead of engaging, I would just go straight to my room. I would have personal, self-development audios playing.

I would still say, "Hey, Dad, how are you doing?" and catch up with him, but afterward I would go right up to my sanctuary, my room with my twin-sized bed and my little cassette player, and that's where I listened to all the tapes and all the books on audio to fill my mind. What I heard and read drowned out all the negative things that I was going to hear anyway, like "David, you need to go get a real job." My dad used to tell me that all the time. Even though he believed in me, he was still telling me I needed to go back to school. But I would still have the positive energy going into my mind because I didn't want anything to terminate the dream that I had...the goal that I had. And what you've got to do is

make your goal so big that yesterday dies. You've got to **surround yourself with people that celebrate your goals** and that encourage you to accomplish your desired success. If you don't have those people around you right now, if you get involved in this industry of network marketing, they're going to encourage you. Especially your upline. They've got a vested interest in making sure you succeed.

That's why you always hear people make suggestions like, "Read this book," or "Listen to this audio," or "Come to this convention or this particular seminar." People will ask you, "What are you talking about? I already went to a convention, why do I have to go to another one? I already read a book, why do I have to read another one? I already listened to an audio, you want me to listen to another one? Come on."

The importance of constantly saturating your consciousness with this type of information cannot be overstated. Repetitious information is really the only way that you're going to be able to drive doubt and limits out of your beliefs. It goes back to deeply understanding the language you speak to give power to your words. The word "information" can be broken down into *in-form-ation*. So the idea goes *in*, it f*orms* and *ation* is the action taken. The information that you're listening to every single day is going to form the actions that you take. Saturate your environment with elements of what your belief system states that you are. It's paramount.

Years and years of listening to books and tapes and audios and reading, these are things that you must do. If you don't have this saturation of this specific type of information coming into your mind...what happens is you listen to yourself—your untrained inner dialogue—and that was one of the mistakes that I was making. I was allowing my untrained inner dialogue to play in my head.

I had to finally take a stand against my inner self's voice. I told myself, "You're broke!" So I was getting advice from a broke person, as opposed to listening to the Earl Nightingales and the Napoleon Hills and my mentor, and those people who have what you want and can now give you the information or advice that you need to take the correct action to be successful. One of the things that I learned from this experience was the importance of raising the bar, raising your beliefs, which will in turn raise your actions, which in turn will raise your result. Believing really takes place when you have the right words. The right words lead you to have the right images in your mind's visualization of your success, but more importantly you have the right emotions. Those emotions have to be in check. They have to match the version of you that has your desire already fulfilled. And those emotions are the emotions of faith, emotions of excitement, enthusiasm. Those things are very important to your success in this business.

LESSON FORTY-FIVE

THE POWER OF READING

MY FAVORITE BOOKS

- *The Magic of Believing* by Claude Bristol
- *Think and Grow Rich* by Napoleon Hill
- *The Strangest Secret* by Earl Nightingale
- *Unlimited Power* by Tony Robbins
- *Building a Network Marketing Business* by Jim Rohn

Two audiobooks that really helped make the shift in believing for me are *Magic of Believing* by Claude Bristol and *The Strangest Secret* by Earl Nightingale. Those are the two books I listened to in audio form that were the most profound to me. I remember sitting down at a leadership event and I had only been involved for about four months and we had about fifty people come.

During a private leadership event, I looked at my mentor and said, "You have the nice car, you have the nice home, you're successful. Why is it that nobody else is like you?" I was really asking facetiously. His response is what has completely put me down this path of where I am today.

He looked at me directly in the eye and said, "Nobody believes the way I do."

I thought to myself, "That's it? You're telling me it's this whole believing thing that brought you your success?"

From that moment forward, I started to study anything that had *anything* to do with believing, I made sure I was listening to an audiobook at all times. So, when I heard the audio version of *The Magic of Believing* and he discussed the mirror technique, talked about the index cards, and he explained the power of suggestion, I began to implement the information given for those techniques. I took action. I never got to meet Claude Bristol; he passed away.

People may hear my story and think, "Oh, I need to be mentored by somebody," but that's not all there is to it. Mentorship is important and helps keep you accountable for your beliefs...but the information that you listen to as soon as you begin to take action can allow you to now attract that mentor. *The Strangest Secret* states that we become what we think about. So that's what I have done. I have presently become what I think about.

The person that I am today exists based on my thoughts. So if I want to change something in my life—whatever it is—all I had to do was change my thoughts. As has been written in the previous lessons in this book, thoughts come from what you perceive with your senses. I believe it comes from God and it comes from the enemy.

Those are the three places that thoughts come from. I knew I could control my five senses. When I taste something, it invokes a thought of, "Oh this tastes good," or "This does not taste good," and my senses react to that thought accordingly by either urging me to eat more, or making me physically repulsed.

When you smell something or touch something, you form thought patterns around the information you're receiving from your senses. I realized I needed to put things around me and create a sensory environment that reflected what I wanted to become. And that realization came to me while listening to the audio of *The Strangest Secret*.

In the very beginning of the audio, he made reference to *The Magic of Believing*. I had listened to that back in 2006! But there I was, years later, after consistently and repetitively being in the right environment and actually being around somebody that was listening to the same audios or had already read the books, and Claude Bristol was suggesting those books to his readers/listeners.

I took his advice and I went back and listened to those two audiobooks, as well as to *25 Secrets of Wealth Creation,* and realized that the author told me what I should be listening to back in 2006. In *25 Secrets of Wealth Creation*, the secret is given right upon beginning to listen to or read the book... it refers the reader to *The Strangest Secret*, but I didn't go seek out *The Strangest Secret* the first time I heard it.

I wouldn't have had to wait until 2009 or 2010 to get the information that is in *The Strangest Secret* if I had been paying attention. I wasn't tuning into the right frequency of my mind's radio of thought patterns. I simply wasn't paying attention.

The reason I implore you to listen to these audios more than once is that your attention may tune in differently—for the better—on a second go. I listened to *The Magic of Believing* for at least five months straight. I didn't listen to any other audio in my headphones or in my car for five entire months. If I was on the phone with someone, doing a three-way call, it was playing in my other ear. I literally held my phone to one ear and had *The Magic of*

Believing playing in my other ear.

Having *The Magic of Believing* constantly looping through my mind was helpful in training me to negate any negativity I received—especially on business calls at that time. This is why repetition is such an important factor in your success. You've got to do it—play the audio and immerse your senses into your desired state—over and over and over and over and over again. If you put *The Magic of Believing* on right now, I could speak it verbatim. If you put *The Strangest Secret* audio on in front of me, I could spit it out word for word.

In 2008, I even played *Think and Win Big* while I was sleeping! That was written by Jerry Clark, Johnny Wimbrey and Les Brown.

The important takeaway from my journey of learning about the power of belief through listening to audiobooks is when you find that information, when you find that specific audio that really speaks to you, you have got to stay on it. You must play it on repeat because of the importance of meditating on your belief day and night, day in and day out.

Have I listened to all of those audios repeatedly? No, I haven't. But once I found one that *really* spoke to me—that gave me information I believed in and could implement—then I played it on repeat in order to master it. Once it has gotten to the point where I probably know the information more thoroughly than the person that actually gave me that audio, or read or wrote the book, then I know I've mastered it.

PARTING WORDS

I have shared a variety of information in *Believe Nation*, from biblical stories to personal triumphs, my own and those of others. You can utilize all given lessons in every aspect of your life. Desire for success looks differently for each individual person, and learning what you truly want to attain is essential for your journey to realizing your dreams. Even our ancient ancestors fundamentally had the same need for success and achieving goals as we do now. We just have different views on what success is because of the society in which we live.

You have to take on the belief that you are secure that the opportunities you want are truly yours. It is a conscious knowing. Yes, you are supposed to immerse yourself in the environment of your desires—sit in the car, visit the house you want, wear the clothes that represent who you want to be—because continuing to look at successful people and materializations of wealth will not get you to where you want to be. You have to make your desires part of your conscious awareness. For example, if you go for a walk, consciously realize you already are the wealthy person you desire to be. Walk as though you've already become the person you see yourself as. From that conscious activity, opportunities will begin to present themselves in your life. It's like you are tuning your radio dial into the station of yourself as successful.

Believe Nation is a tool for you to anchor your belief in your ability to be that which you desire to be. Use the Believe Nation platform and this book as your guide. You will not fail if you implement true faith, true belief, and action toward your personal success.